Dream Interpretation

A Spiritual Guide to Symbols, Words, Themes, and Meanings of Dreams

© Copyright 2024 – All rights reserved.

The content contained within this book may not be reproduced, duplicated or transmitted without direct written permission from the author or the publisher.

Under no circumstances will any blame or legal responsibility be held against the publisher, or author, for any damages, reparation, or monetary loss due to the information contained within this book, either directly or indirectly.

Legal Notice:

This book is copyright protected. It is only for personal use. You cannot amend, distribute, sell, use, quote or paraphrase any part, or the content within this book, without the consent of the author or publisher.

Disclaimer Notice:

Please note the information contained within this document is for educational and entertainment purposes only. All effort has been executed to present accurate, up to date, reliable, complete information. No warranties of any kind are declared or implied. Readers acknowledge that the author is not engaging in the rendering of legal, financial, medical or professional advice. The content within this book has been derived from various sources. Please consult a licensed professional before attempting any techniques outlined in this book.

By reading this document, the reader agrees that under no circumstances is the author responsible for any losses, direct or indirect, that are incurred as a result of the use of information contained within this document, including, but not limited to, errors, omissions, or inaccuracies.

Your Free Gift
(only available for a limited time)

Thanks for getting this book! If you want to learn more about various spirituality topics, then join Mari Silva's community and get a free guided meditation MP3 for awakening your third eye. This guided meditation mp3 is designed to open and strengthen ones third eye so you can experience a higher state of consciousness. Simply visit the link below the image to get started.

https://spiritualityspot.com/meditation

Table of Contents

INTRODUCTION 1
CHAPTER 1: WHY DO WE DREAM? 3
CHAPTER 2: REMEMBER YOUR DREAMS AND LOOK FOR PATTERNS 13
CHAPTER 3: WHAT ARE YOU DOING IN YOUR DREAM? 23
CHAPTER 4: DREAM LOCATIONS AND MEANINGS 33
CHAPTER 5: DREAM SYMBOLISM OF THE FOUR ELEMENTS 42
CHAPTER 6: LOOKING AT COLORS AND NUMBERS 53
CHAPTER 7: DREAMS WITH ANIMALS AND PLANTS 65
CHAPTER 8: DREAMS ABOUT BODY PARTS 76
CHAPTER 9: WHEN SUPERNATURAL BEINGS APPEAR 85
CHAPTER 10: ADVANCED DREAM INTERPRETATION TECHNIQUES 94
GLOSSARY OF DREAM SYMBOLS 102
CONCLUSION 109
HERE'S ANOTHER BOOK BY MARI SILVA THAT YOU MIGHT LIKE 111
YOUR FREE GIFT (ONLY AVAILABLE FOR A LIMITED TIME) 112
BIBLIOGRAPHY 113

Introduction

Due to their elusive and mysterious nature, dreams have always interested people. Since ancient times, different civilizations have wondered why people dream and what these dreams could mean. They recorded their interpretations and used dream symbolism for healing, divination, and guidance. At the beginning of the twentieth century, people started to take a more scientific approach to dream interpretation. From this book, you will learn the different theories about the role of dream symbolism in psychoanalysis and how these can be incorporated into traditional beliefs about dreams.

While there is no clear answer to whether a dream means anything, looking into your dream—including its elements and circumstances—can give you a better idea of how to interpret it. Sometimes, the information you uncover about yourself in your sleep is far more substantial than what you learn during waking hours. Dreams can echo consolidated memories you have had, stimuli your brain has trouble processing in REM sleep, and much more. To find a connection between your dream state and waking life, you'll need to start by taking note of what you've experienced in your dreams—and this book will help you through comprehensive explanations and beginner-friendly practical advice.

For example, your dreams can involve specific actions, locations, elements, colors, or numbers. You can also have recurring dreams about body parts, plants, animals, and even supernatural beings. From spiritual guides to fairies and dwarves, there is no limit to what your imagination can conjure up in your dreams. The book has chapters dedicated to all these possible dream elements, discussing their meanings, variations, and significance in waking life. Still, since dreams stem from the subconscious mind, no symbol can have definitive, universal importance. In the last chapter, you'll learn a few advanced dream interpretation techniques to provide more detailed insight into your dreams and their connection to your waking life.

The key to a successful dream interpretation is to avoid interpreting them literally. While the symbols can hint at which direction you should be heading with your analysis, what truly matters is your emotional connection to your dreams. Decoding the emotions each dream evokes allows you to expand your consciousness. Your dreams are extensions of the subconscious mind, and you are increasing your emotional and spiritual awareness with each dream you interpret. Creating a conscious mental catalog of the meaning of your dreams is like learning a new language. And just like when learning a new language, you embark on a rewarding journey. Read on if you're ready to start deciphering your dreams and earning the ultimate rewards that come with them.

Chapter 1: Why Do We Dream?

Dreams are a mystery humanity has been exploring since the dawn of time. This chapter is designed to answer the question posed in the title from the perspective of various fields of study: Scientific, psychological, religious, and spiritual. It will define the dream interpretation concept and explore its historical and cultural context and benefits. You will also learn about the different types of dreams.

The Concept of Dream Interpretation

The origins of dream interpretation can be traced back to 3000-4000 B.C. to ancient Babylon and Samaria. These civilizations used clay tablets to record people's dreams and interpret their possible meanings. While nothing tangible supports this, historians believe that the Sumerians and the Babylonians believed that dreams were the extension of real life. Some archeological evidence suggests that the Sumerians saw the dream realm as a far more powerful world than the waking one. They saw dreams as a way to liberate and empower themselves because all things are possible in dreams, and a person can do more than they can in real life.

In ancient Greece and ancient Rome, troops heading to the battlefield were often accompanied by dream interpreters who tried to discern the upcoming fight's outcome based on the warriors' dreams. They considered dreams as messages from the gods, often formulated as orders people had to follow.

In ancient Egypt, Pharos and other leaders also relied on dream interpretation when making critical decisions. The Egyptian interpreters recorded people's dreams in hieroglyphics. If someone had particularly vivid dreams or events in their dreams that affected their waking life, they were believed to be blessed by the gods. Dream interpreters were held in high regard as they were said to be divinely gifted by the gods.

The Bible has over 700 references to dreams and their significance in the waking world.

A prophecy was one of the biggest reasons dream interpretation was widespread in all different cultures. Most of the time, people analyze dreams for signs of warnings about the future. Whatever the source of the warning messages, they were seen as hints about future events. Even better, people discovered that dreams offered advice on what to do or avoid when challenging situations arose. At other times, dreams were messages from evil spirits, demons, and other creatures—threats people were made aware of and advised to protect themselves against in their sleep.

Dream interpretations were also used for medicinal purposes, especially in ancient China and ancient Greece. They could help establish a proper diagnosis and treatment plan for an illness and determine what was wrong with the dreamer's body or mind.

The ancient Chinese believed dreams were souls of resting people expressing their desires. According to the Chinese, after the body fell asleep, the soul left it and ventured into the dream realm. People were warned not to suddenly wake someone, as this could cause their souls to remain trapped in the dream world. Even contemporary Chinese people choose to wake up naturally and avoid using alarm locks.

Mexican and Native American tribes also view dreams as the dimension of a soul. Their ancestors live in the dream world, appearing as other living forms, like plants or animals. They use the dream world to visit and communicate with ancestral spirits. In dreams, the ancestors can help answer questions, share wisdom about life, and offer guidance for finding one's path.

Later on, the popularity of dream interpretation diminished drastically—and by the nineteenth century, dreams were dismissed as signifiers of real-life events. Dreams were attributed to indigestion, anxiety, or a noisy environment at night. It was not until the early twentieth century that dream analysis was revived by Austrian psychoanalyst Sigmund Freud.

While treating mental illnesses, Freud realized that his patients' dreams had significance when finding the treatment for their condition. By analyzing their dreams, he helped patients understand the cause of their mental health issues. He believed that by using the information the patients revealed in their dream, he could find a way to cure or manage their symptoms.

Ever since then, this discipline has grown increasingly popular. Soon after Freud, other psychoanalysts and medical professionals became interested in dream interpretation. Ann Faraday, the author of the novel *The Dream Game*, writes about many dream interpretation techniques. Nowadays, dream research continues to grow. However, researchers often encounter a common problem: How to memorize dream images. Unless people find their dreams intellectually stimulating, joyful, or inspiring, they often forget what they dream about the moment they wake up.

Others believe your dreams can reveal more about yourself than the meaning of the dream itself. This is based on a modern scientific approach, which suggests that dreams are the brain's response to external stimuli, which the organ cannot process during waking hours. This contradicts the popular theory of dreams being the gateway for hidden desires. Another issue with dream interpretation is that you are more likely to remember your dreams if they revolve around adverse events or circumstances surrounding people you dislike. While you can also retain dreams related to loved ones and other positive dreams, the percentage is far less than retained negative dreams. This means that you will likely interpret dreams so that they can support your beliefs about your environment, yourself, and other people.

People who often rely on dream interpretation for orientation in day-to-day life can view their dreams as a self-fulfilling prophecy. For example, a dream about not performing well in a job interview—you'll be either too stressed to showcase your best skills or less motivated to prepare well for the interview.

Theories about Dream Symbolism

Dream interpretation plays a crucial role in psychoanalysis. Due to this, several analysts have developed theories about dreams and their meanings. Sigmund Freud and Carl Jung were two leading psychoanalysts who found dream images compelling to analyze and use as therapeutic tools.

At the beginning of the twentieth century, most scientists were not concerned about attaching too many meanings to people's dreams. Most of them assumed that dream images were by-products of the brain processing information during the REM phase of sleep. Some scientists even support this theory today, and non-professionals guided by their theories often dismiss unfavorable dream events. After all, how many times have you heard someone describing their bad dream images as silly dreams? Freud, on the other hand, noticed early on that his patients' dreams were meaningful—regardless of how little a person remembered from their dreams or how little their dream images meant to the particular person.

Freud affirmed that with research, professionals could develop procedures for successful dream interpretation. He began by laying the foundation with his dream interpretation theory. He found that the key to interpreting dreams more effectively was simply letting the person describe whatever details they could remember. This prompted people to follow their trains of thought rather than being influenced by how the professional interprets them. They could form their own ideas of what their dreams could have meant.

By practicing free association (between dream images and the thoughts they evoke), Freud found that there were four elements in dream work. The first one is condensation. It is referred to as the piling up of several ideas in one dream—as the information of all these ideas was pulled into one thought and shown as one dream picture. The second element is displacement, which is associated with hidden emotional meanings. This often happens when the dreamer confuses significant and meaningless parts of their dreams. The third is symbolization, which points to repressed ideas only shown as items that symbolize their meaning. Secondary revision is the fourth element. It denotes the reorganization of dreams, which makes them easier to understand and remember.

Most people focus on what they can consciously remember from their dreams. However, as Freud—and later Jung—agreed, dreams are more of a sorting process for the brain for all daytime experiences. This affects how the brain functions and why it hides some parts of the dream world in the subconscious. People's brains are constantly changing due to their subconscious content, evolving to accommodate the type of information the brain gathers and processes. Mentored by Freud, Jung also found allies in dreams when treating mental conditions. Freud and Jung brought more in-depth insights into dream interpretation from the science of their era and other ancient sources, including history, mythology, and art. Their work helped them amass significant knowledge about the human psyche. This, in turn, enabled the next generation of dream interpreters and psychoanalysts to understand the nature of dreams and how they interact with the body and mind.

Their agreement and cooperation notwithstanding, there were fundamental differences between Jung's and Freud's theories about dream interpretation. Whereas his mentor looked into the past causes of dreams, Jung's work was focused on the future implication of dreams. He considered dream images critical to reveal information about the patient's health development in the future. He established several functions for the dreams. The primary was compensation—which he called the brain's way of maintaining the balance between conscious and subconscious ideas. According to Jung, if a conscious person tries to repress their subconscious thoughts, their dreams will show the imbalance and prompt them to return to their balanced self.

The second function of dreams—according to Jung—is reductive compensation. This is a unique form of Jung's compensation. It's a more severe attempt from one's dreams to reinstate the balance lost due to the inflated conscious ego that tries to control everything in waking life. Jung believed that dreams can always tell a person who they are and who they have the potential to be. If you have an opinion about yourself that does not reflect reality, the dreams will have you face the truth. They will compensate for your mistaken beliefs by showing you images that contradict your ideas about yourself. They bring you back into the depths of your psyche, allowing you to develop a more accurate self-picture. For example, if you think your actions always reflect great morals—even if they do not—your dreams will likely remind you of all your thoughts, emotions, and actions that point to faulty morals.

The prospective function of a dream is yet another one determined by Jung. While he believed most dreams could fulfill the first two functions, he didn't exclude the possibility of dream images having other purposes. He proposed a third fundamental function of dreams: The prospective function. This is very similar to the prophetic ideas traditional religious systems have about dreams. Prospective dreams offer glimpses into potential future events. According to Jung, the role of this function is to help a person's growth and guide them on their path toward achieving integration and balance. If people can learn to interpret these prophetic dreams, they can access a unique pool of wisdom hidden in their subconscious minds.

Types of Dreams

While it is still unclear how many dreams people can have, there is a universal estimation of the number. Below are the most common dream types.

Daydreams

Most people would describe daydreaming as having vivid visions during waking hours. These visions are associated with hidden desires, fantasies, or unfulfilled expectations. At other times, they may be desired outcomes of potential situations or reveries of past occurrences. Daydreams are more common than you think. They are also more easily remembered than the dreams from sleeping hours—although most people dismiss them faster than any other type of dream.

Epic Dreams

These dreams are vivid dreams that, true to their names, are too epic to forget. They are one of the most interpreted dream forms, even though it takes some work to pin down their meaning. Interpreters consider these as profound experiences with long-standing effects and, depending on whether you adhere to their message, have the potential to change your life. The condition called epic dream disorder causes people to have these memorable dreams in their sleep without any emotional meaning. These excessive dreams typically involve people doing day-to-day tasks in their dreams until they become so tired that they wake up exhausted in the morning.

False Awakening Dreams

Some people go through their morning routine in their dream thinking they are already awake—when, in fact, they're still profoundly asleep. This is called a false awakening, resulting from a transition from REM sleep to the light sleep phase. REM sleep is responsible for mental health recovery, so these dreams are a way of your mind preparing you mentally for the day ahead. False awakenings are linked to lucid dreams.

Nightmares

People abruptly wake up from sleep due to their overwhelming effect.
https://unsplash.com/photos/j8a-TEakg78?utm_source=unsplash&utm_medium=referral&utm_content=creditShareLink

Nightmares are described as disturbing or downright frightening dreams showcasing images laced with negative emotions, like despair, fear, disgust, sadness, or a combination of these emotions. Due to their overwhelming effect, nightmares cause most people to wake up suddenly. However, they may typically dismiss it as a normal occurrence. In rare cases, nightmares become so intense that they disturb a person's sleep and waking life. Commonly occurring vivid nightmares can have a detrimental effect on your cognitive functions.

Night Terrors

Night terrors are similar to nightmares, except they're accompanied by sounds and movements a person makes while sleeping. They're the most common in older children and adolescents; however, a small percentage of adults also have them regularly. Some night terrors involve a person making only a few movements and sounds. Others cause them to scream and flail for several minutes or even longer.

Progressive Dreams

Due to their unique nature, progressive dreams are still uncharted territory. Interpreters define them as a sequence of images with a continuous narrative. Essentially, you are experiencing a story unfolding as you keep dreaming about the same thing. The dreams can follow each other nightly, like continuously reading a book or sporadically watching a new series on TV and waiting for the still-to-come episodes.

Lucid Dreams

Lucid dreams are rarely recorded. They involve a person being suspended between the dream state and conscious wakefulness. Interestingly enough, some people retain the awareness and the ability to control their dream. Others can even communicate consciously in lucid dreams. Dream interpreters suggest that, through practice and discipline, it is possible to train yourself to have a lucid dream.

Prophetic Dreams

Prophetic dreams have brought the fascination of dream interpretation into people's lives. For centuries, people have believed dreams can predict the future. Some people are inclined to prophetic dreams and can analyze and interpret them effortlessly. They can use precognition for guidance, healing, warning, and other purposes to manifest more detailed outcomes.

Recurring Dreams

Recurring dreams are the replay of the same dream images. They often reflect an unresolved issue, unmet desire, or the brain's struggle to process traumatic experiences during waking hours. Sometimes recurring dreams only involve one particular image, whereas, on other occasions, you will see the repeat of an entire dream sequence. The dreams can continue until the cause is resolved or replaced with something else.

Vivid Dreams

Vivid dreams are caused by a condition called REM rebound, which is related to mental health recovery. This is your mind's way of compensating for being sleep-deprived because of stress or other factors. During REM, you experience heightened brain activity, which creates vivid dreams. These dreams are also common when people have a high fever, which hinders the brain's ability to regulate its activity during sleep.

The Benefits of Dream Interpretation

Learning to analyze and comprehend your dreams takes some time and practice. As you embark on this journey, you will notice that while some dream images can be discerned effortlessly, most will be far more complex. Whether you rely only on your intuition or use the help of known dream symbols will be up to you. However, it will be easier to help you get started if you know the benefits of dream interpretation.

Here are see several advantages of dream work to inspire you to commence this journey:

- Dreams can help you find yourself. If you are struggling to find your path, your dreams can steer you in the right direction.
- Dreams can help you stay healthy. By warning you about future health, your dreams can help you prevent illnesses by seeking help and adopting a healthier lifestyle.
- Dreams can keep you safe. Many people receive warnings about environmental events in dreams, which help them escape dangerous situations.
- Dreams will not let you deny the truth. They show you an issue as it is, enabling you to learn the truth of every situation. While sobering, a healthy dose of dream reality is necessary for a happy life.
- Dreams can provide solutions for real-life issues. Sometimes, the only way your mind can work through a problem is to pull out a solution from the subconscious and show it to you in your dreams.
- Dreams show how you feel about people, events, and situations. If you have any pent-up feelings you leave to fester in your waking life, dreams can help release them, preventing them from causing further disturbances in your life and health.
- Dreams help build better relationships. Your dreams can warn you about red flags in a relationship you would otherwise ignore due to emotional involvement. They can help you eliminate toxic people from your life, so you can focus on building a connection with people who contribute positively to your life. Dreams can also help you identify the right romantic partner, the best ways to resolve issues in your relationships, build

harmony, and keep your love life enjoyable for you and your partner.
- Dreams can help you communicate with your ancestors. Departed loved ones can visit you in your dreams, leaving you messages—but you'll only know they have done this if you take your time to learn dream interpretation. This ancient art will help you reveal the difference between spiritual messages and messages coming from your subconscious.
- Dreams will show you your future. They can help you glimpse into future outcomes based on current actions. This lets you decide whether to continue on your current path or change course to get a different outcome.
- Dreams are the key to spiritual and mental growth. The messages you receive in your dreams can reflect the information you need to become a better person or obtain the spiritual enlightenment you desire.
- Dreams offer peace of mind. If nothing else, interpreting your dreams will have a therapeutic effect on your mental health. By showing you what your conscious mind struggles with, you're gaining an insight into the causation of your symptoms. After learning where they come from, it will be much easier to chase away anxiety and other symptoms.

Chapter 2: Remember Your Dreams and Look for Patterns

Dreams can be mysterious, fascinating, and sometimes even terrifying. They can bring you to unknown places, introduce unfamiliar faces, and present bizarre scenarios that often leave you wondering what they mean. They have been the topic of numerous discussions, debates, and interpretations across different cultures and civilizations. However, one of the biggest challenges that people face when trying to interpret their dreams is remembering them.

How often have you woken up in the morning, unable to recall a single detail of what you dreamed the night before? The frustrating feeling of knowing that you had a dream but not being able to remember it can be quite common. But why does this happen? The science behind why people struggle to remember their dreams still needs to be fully understood. However, it has something to do with the fact that dreams occur during the Rapid Eye Movement (REM) stage of sleep, which is the deepest stage, so it is even more challenging to remember the details of your dreams.

Despite these challenges, remembering your dreams can be incredibly helpful in gaining insight into your subconscious mind. By paying attention to recurring themes, symbols, and emotions in your dreams, you can unravel their meaning and better understand your inner self. This chapter will provide various techniques to help you improve your dream recall, like keeping a dream journal and creating a bedtime routine.

Why You Have Trouble Remembering Dreams

During a typical sleep cycle, the brain goes through several stages of sleep. These stages are categorized into two main types: Non-Rapid Eye Movement (NREM) sleep and Rapid Eye Movement (REM) sleep. NREM sleep has three stages, while REM sleep constitutes only one stage. REM sleep is known as the deepest stage of sleep, as it is associated with a high level of brain activity and increased physiological responses. During this time, the brain becomes more active, and the body experiences changes in heart rate, blood pressure, and respiration. It is also during this stage that people have most of their dreams.

Although REM sleep is a vital part of the sleep cycle, it's challenging to remember your dreams. The brain is more active during REM sleep, and the body is in a state of deep relaxation, making it more difficult to recall the details of the dream. Additionally, REM sleep occurs toward the end of the sleep cycle, which means that when you wake up, you are more likely to remember the dreams you had earlier in the night, during the lighter stages of sleep, than those that occurred during the REM stage. Furthermore, the brain processes and stores memories during sleep; however, this can be interrupted by the REM stage, leading to difficulty with recall. The memories formed during REM sleep may be more challenging to retrieve as the brain is more active, and there is a higher level of neural activity, making it harder to separate memories from dreams.

Techniques to Enhance Your Sleep Recall

Sleep recall, or the ability to remember your dreams, can be an elusive phenomenon for many people. However, with a few simple techniques, you can improve your recall and unlock the hidden world of your dreams. Here are some techniques to help you improve your sleep recall:

1. Keep a Dream Journal

Keeping a dream journal will train your brain to remember your dreams more vividly.
https://unsplash.com/photos/fVUl6kzIvLg?utm_source=unsplash&utm_medium=referral&utm_content=creditShareLink

Keep a notebook near your bed and write down your dreams as soon as you wake up. This practice can help you train your brain to remember your dreams more vividly. Dream journaling can include these steps:

Step 1: Choose a Journal

Choosing a dedicated journal for your dreams helps you stay organized and consistent. You can use a physical journal or an app on your phone or computer. Choose one that you like and find easy to use. Consider using a hardcover journal or one with sturdy binding that can withstand frequent use. Plus, you can decorate your journal to make the process more appealing.

Step 2: Record the Dream

Start each dream entry with the date, including the day of the week. This helps you track your dreams and identify patterns. Write down everything you remember about the dream, including colors, emotions, people, and events. Be as specific and detailed as possible, using descriptive language. This can help you capture the essence of the dream and remember it more vividly. Try to write down the dream as soon as you wake up—before getting out of bed or doing anything else. This will help you remember more details.

Step 3: Underline Key Elements

As you write, underline or highlight the main themes, recurring objects, or people in your dreams. This will give insight into your subconscious mind. For example, if you often dream about flying, underline "flying" or "wings" in your dream entries. You can use a different color pen or highlighter to underline key elements. This makes them stand out and easier to find later.

Step 4: Add Context

If possible, write down any context relevant to the dream, such as your mood before going to bed or any events that happened during the day. This can help you understand why you had the dream and what it may mean. Use abbreviations or shorthand for context information to save time and space. For example, you could use "Mood: Anxious" or "Event: Meeting with boss."

Step 5: Reflect on the Dream

After recording the dream, take a moment to reflect on its meaning or any insights it might offer. You can also write down any questions you have about the dream. This can help you understand the dream on a deeper level and uncover its underlying messages. Write down your initial reactions and feelings about the dream, and capture your initial impressions and insights.

Step 6: Repeat

Make a habit of recording your dreams every morning, even if you do not remember much at first. Over time, this practice will help you train your brain to remember details and dreams more easily. Set aside a specific time each morning to record your dreams, such as right after waking up or during your morning routine. This can help you establish a consistent habit. Consider using a reward system to motivate yourself to record your dreams regularly. For example, you could reward yourself with a small treat or activity each time you record a dream for a certain number of days in a row.

2. Use the 5Ws Technique

The 5Ws method is a simplified approach to dream recall that focuses on answering the five basic questions: Who? What? When? Where? and why? It is a great option for people who have less time to keep a detailed dream journal.

Step 1: Write Down the Five Questions

On a piece of paper or your digital format, write down the five questions: Who? What? When? Where? and Why? Leave enough space under each question to write your answers. Use a consistent format for the questions, such as all caps or bold text, to make them stand out.

Step 2: Recall the Dream

Think back to your dream and try to remember as many details as possible. Focus on answering the five questions with as much information as you can recall.

Step 3: Answer the Questions

Under each question, write down your answers. Be as specific using descriptive language.

- <u>Who?</u> Write down any people or characters who appeared in the dream, including yourself and others.
- <u>What?</u> Write down any events, actions, or objects that appeared in the dream.
- <u>When?</u> Write down any time-related details, such as the time of day or how much time seemed to pass in the dream.
- <u>Where?</u> Write down any locations or settings that appeared in the dream, including any changes in location.
- <u>Why?</u> Write down any emotions, motivations, or reasons that might have contributed to the dream.

If you cannot remember an answer to a question, leave it blank and move on. You can always come back to it later if you remember more details.

3. Practice Lucid Dreaming

Lucid dreaming is the ability to control your dreams consciously. By practicing lucid dreaming, you can become more aware of your dreams, making it easier to remember them later.

Step 1: Set Your Intention

Before you go to bed, set your intention to have a lucid dream. Repeat affirmations like "*I will become aware that I am dreaming*" or "*I will have a lucid dream tonight*" to help your subconscious mind prepare for the experience.

Step 2: Reality Checks

Throughout the day, take reality checks to increase your awareness of whether you are dreaming. Ask yourself questions like *"Am I dreaming right now?"* and perform actions like looking at your hands, which can appear distorted or unusual in dreams.

Step 3: Induce Lucid Dreaming

There are several techniques you can use to induce lucid dreaming. Some popular methods include:

- <u>Wake-Back-to-Bed (WBTB) Technique:</u> Set an alarm to wake up after five or six hours of sleep and stay awake for thirty to 60 minutes before returning to bed. This technique increases your chances of having a lucid dream.
- <u>Mnemonic Induction of Lucid Dreams (MILD) Technique:</u> Before going to sleep, repeat a phrase like *"I will have a lucid dream tonight"* while visualizing yourself becoming lucid in a dream. This technique programs your subconscious to induce lucid dreaming.
- <u>Wake-Initiated Lucid Dream (WILD) Technique:</u> This involves staying awake while your body falls asleep. Lie down in a comfortable position and focus on your breathing or a simple mental image. As your body falls asleep, you may enter a lucid dream.

Step 4: Stay Calm and Engage with the Dream

Once you realize you're in a lucid dream, stay calm and engage with the dream. You can try different things like flying, talking to dream characters, or exploring your dream world. The more you engage with the dream, the longer you will stay in a lucid state.

Step 5: Exit the Dream

When you're ready to wake up, try to exit the dream gently. You can try closing your eyes and imagining yourself waking up in bed or simply letting the dream fade away.

4. Create a Dream Map

Create a visual map of your dreams using images, symbols, and colors. This can help you remember your dreams more vividly and connect with their emotions and themes.

Step 1: Gather Your Materials

Collect art supplies like colored pencils, markers, and paper. You can also add images from magazines or printouts from the internet to your map.

Step 2: Set the Scene

Start by drawing a landscape or setting that represents your dream world. This can be a cityscape, forest, or any other environment you recall from your dreams.

Step 3: Add Symbols and Images

Think about the characters, objects, and events that appeared in your dream and draw or cut out images that represent them. Use symbols and colors that feel meaningful, even if they do not match the objects exactly.

Step 4: Connect the Dots

As you add more symbols and images to your map, look for connections between them. Are there recurring themes or emotions? Are certain objects or characters always present together? Draw lines or arrows to connect these elements.

Step 5: Reflect on Your Map

Once you have finished your dream map, reflect on what you've created for a few moments. What themes or emotions are present? Are there any surprises or insights that you gained from the process?

Step 6: Use Your Dream Map

Keep your dream map in a visible place where you can see it regularly, like on your bedroom wall or in your journal. Use it as a tool for dream recall and reflection, and add to it as you have new dreams. The more you engage with your dream map, the more vivid and meaningful your dreams may become.

5. Visualize Your Dreams

Use guided visualization techniques to help you remember and explore your dreams in more detail. Imagine yourself back in the dream, and ask yourself questions about what you experienced. This can help you unlock hidden meanings and insights from your dreams.

Step 1: Relax Your Mind and Body

Find a quiet, comfortable place where you will not be disturbed. Close your eyes, take a few deep breaths, and allow your body to relax. You can also listen to calming music or guided meditation recordings to help you relax.

Step 2: Recall Your Dream

Think back to a recent dream that you want to explore further. Remember as many details as possible, including the setting, characters, and events.

Step 3: Visualize Yourself in the Dream

Imagine yourself back in the dream as if you were watching it unfold before your eyes. Visualize the setting and characters as vividly as you can. Try to engage all your senses, noticing any sounds, smells, or textures you can recall.

Step 4: Ask Questions

As you visualize yourself in the dream, ask yourself questions about what you are experiencing. For example, you could ask, "What does this character represent?" or "What is the significance of this object?" Use your intuition and imagination to explore different interpretations and meanings.

Step 5: Reflect on Your Insights

After you have spent some time exploring your dream through visualization, take a few moments to reflect on any insights or revelations that you gained. Write them down in a dream journal, along with any lingering questions or mysteries.

6. Use Dream Art

Create art inspired by your dreams, such as paintings, drawings, or collages. This helps you to connect with the emotions and themes of your dreams and bring them to life in a tangible way.

Painting or drawing your expression of what you dream about can be therapeutic.
https://unsplash.com/photos/FwF_fKj5tBo

Step 1: Set Up Your Art Supplies

Gather your art supplies, such as pencils, markers, watercolors, or digital tools. Have a sketchbook or piece of paper ready to work on.

Step 2: Think about Your Dream

Take a moment to focus on the dream you want to remember. What images or symbols stand out? What colors or emotions are associated with the dream? You can also look at any notes or journals you have kept about the dream.

Step 3: Start Creating

Use your art supplies to create a visual representation of your dream. This can be a realistic drawing, an abstract painting, or even a collage of images and symbols. Focus on capturing the essence of the dream rather than trying to recreate it exactly.

Step 4: Add Details and Descriptions

As you work on your dream art, write down any details or descriptions that come to mind. This helps you remember the dream more clearly and make connections between different elements.

Step 5: Reflect on Your Dream Art

Take some time to reflect on the dream art you've created. What emotions or insights does it bring up? Are there any patterns or themes that emerge? Write down any thoughts or reflections in your dream journal.

7. Dream Sharing

Before bed, focus on specific dream cues or triggers, such as a recurring dream symbol or a particular emotion. This can increase your chances of recognizing these cues in your dreams and help you remember more details.

Step 1: Choose a Trusted Friend or Family Member

You want to make sure that you feel comfortable being vulnerable with them and that they will provide positive feedback and support.

Step 2: Set Aside Time

Set aside time to talk about your dreams regularly. This could be once a week or every few weeks, depending on your schedule and availability. Find a time that works for both you and your dream-sharing partner.

Step 3: Recollect Your Dreams

Before your scheduled time to share, ensure you clearly recollect your dreams. Keep your dream journal beside your bed and write down as many details as you can remember upon waking up.

Step 4: Share

When it is time to share, start by giving an overview of the dream, including any emotions, themes, or important details that stood out to you. Be descriptive and use specific language.

Step 5: Get Insight

Listen to your dream-sharing partner's feedback and insights. Ask questions and clarify any points that are not clear. Be open to different perspectives and interpretations of your dreams.

Remembering your dreams can be a valuable tool for personal growth, self-discovery, and creativity. Dreams can provide insights into your subconscious mind and offer solutions to problems you may be struggling with in your waking life. By making a conscious effort to remember and analyze dreams, you can gain a deeper understanding of yourself and the world around you. In addition to the mentioned techniques, relaxation exercises such as meditation or deep breathing can quieten the mind and promote a deeper sleep, resulting in more vivid dreams.

It's also important to note that not all dreams hold significant meanings or symbolism. Some dreams may simply reflect your daily experiences or result from random neural firings during sleep. Therefore, it's essential to approach dream interpretation with an open mind and not get too caught up in trying to find meaning in every dream. It's also worth mentioning that everyone's dreams are unique to them. Personal experiences, cultural background, and individual beliefs can influence dreams. Therefore, while there may be some universal symbols and archetypes, it's crucial to remember that the interpretation of a dream is ultimately up to the dreamer.

Chapter 3: What Are You Doing in Your Dream?

Dreams often mimic real life. Everything you see and experience in your waking life can find its way into your dreams. When you close your eyes to sleep at night, you usually see yourself doing activities like running, eating, or laughing, while in other dreams, you see some of your worst fears realized, like falling from the sky or drowning. However, with dreams, everything has a different meaning.

This chapter will discuss everyday actions and activities you see in your dreams and what they symbolize.

Drowning

Drowning is one of the worst nightmares, yet has positive and negative meanings. It can indicate that you are overwhelmed in your waking life and need a break. The dream can also mean that you are under a lot of stress and feel like you are drowning and need to catch your breath. Since water is associated with rebirth, it can symbolize renewal, new beginnings, and transformation.

Dreaming of drowning can have negative and positive interpretations.
https://www.pexels.com/photo/hands-of-crop-faceless-man-under-water-7457629/

Avoiding Drowning

If you save yourself from drowning, it indicates you can avoid harmful situations that can impact your spiritual, physical, and mental well-being. Even if you face challenges and obstacles, you will overcome them and come out stronger. It also means that good luck is coming your way, so you should be prepared.

Dying by Drowning

If you drown and die in your dream, it is a sign that you are unable to cope with your inhibitions and emotions. Thus, you need to change your mindset and start adopting a positive attitude toward your life.

Drowning in a Swimming Boat

Since pools are human-made, dreaming that you are drowning in one indicates that someone in your circle is causing you trouble or that you are the one making things hard for yourself. You have probably set unattainable goals for yourself and cannot accomplish them. It can also mean a close friend you trust is causing your problems. They could be jealous and spiteful and have no problem betraying you.

Drowning on a Boat

In dreams, boats symbolize the course you are taking in your life. If you dream you are on a sinking boat, you are about to face challenges in your waking life. You are under a lot of stress, and this dream is telling you to slow down. You are probably feeling exhausted in your waking life or feel anxious about your life at the moment. If you are steering the boat while it is sinking, nothing is going right in your life.

Seeing a Loved One Drowning

Dreaming of a loved one drowning suggests you are afraid to lose them. You are worried about someone in your life who could be dying or struggling with health issues.

Seeing Yourself Drowning

If you are the one drowning, you are experiencing negative emotions in real life, like anxiety, fear, or depression. You feel that you are making yourself miserable and can do nothing to change your situation.

Eating

Eating dreams are usually pleasant unless you are eating something inedible. This dream could simply mean that you went to bed hungry or are on a diet and craving a certain type of food, like pizza or chocolate. However, this dream can have other different meanings. It is not just the act of eating; the food and taste can also have meanings. If the food tastes strange, you missed a big opportunity in your waking life. Experiencing the food's texture, sensation, and taste in the dream means you are ambitious and driven to succeed.

Eating can symbolize a hunger for something missing in your life, like love, recognition, or a better career. It can suggest there is a goal you want or are excited about and cannot wait to accomplish, like buying a new car or losing weight. How you eat your food in your dream represents how much you want to achieve this goal.

Eating Alone

Dreaming about eating alone can signify several things.
https://unsplash.com/photos/Orz90t6o0e4?utm_source=unsplash&utm_medium=referral&utm_content=creditShareLink

Eating alone in your dream indicates you feel lost or isolated from the people in your life. However, if you feel happy or relaxed during your meal, you require some peace and quiet in your waking life.

If you are unhappy while eating alone in your dream, you feel lonely and should do something to conquer this feeling.

Eating Something Inedible

Not all eating dreams are about food. Eating something inedible means that you do not know how to deal with the problems in your life, and you need to confront them right away.

Eating with Others

Eating with other people in your dreams has a more positive meaning than eating alone. It shows your comfort in social situations and that you have a great relationship with the people in your life. It can also mean you desire to connect with others or lack friendships.

Lack of Food

Lack of food or not having enough food in your dream indicates that something is missing in your life. You can also be hungry for new experiences. You are doing something in your life that does not bring you any satisfaction, or you have achieved a goal you have been working on for a long time, but you still feel unhappy.

Overeating

Overeating in your dream means you are overwhelmed in your waking life. You are under a lot of stress, and you need a break. It can also indicate that you're feeling insecure and need to impress someone or are trying to get a person you are interested in to notice you. The dream can also signify that you need a change in your life.

Poisonous Food

Poisonous food means you're struggling with a problem in your waking life. Someone close to you has disappointed you, or a job or experience you had high hopes for made you miserable. It can also mean you're working hard to achieve a goal but are nowhere near accomplishing it and feel hopeless.

Falling

Falling dreams are common and unpleasant, and they usually have different meanings. They can symbolize a lack of control over various issues in your life, which lead to anxiety, fear, and helplessness. Interpreting this dream depends on finding clues within the context of your dream.

Falling dreams are one of the most common.
https://www.pexels.com/photo/a-falling-woman-wearing-a-sheer-dress-5655150/

Dreaming of Someone Else Falling

This dream means you are worried about losing someone you care about, like your partner leaving you. It also indicates that a loved one is struggling with control in their life, and you're worried about them.

Falling Down an Elevator

Dreaming you are falling down an elevator or stairs symbolizes poor emotional well-being and low self-confidence. You could also be worried that things are changing around you and you cannot keep up with others. This dream also means that you're emotionally hurt. If you manage to get out of the elevator or someone saves you, new opportunities are coming your way.

Falling into the Darkness

Falling into an unknown place or a dark abyss means that you are afraid of something in real life. Your dream is telling you to confront these fears right away. If this is a recurrent dream, see what clues or messages it is giving you and re-evaluate your life to see what you need to address. Fear of the unknown and the future is usually the main trigger behind this dream.

Getting Hurt

Dreaming that you fell and got hurt means you are unable to confront certain aspects of yourself and your life, like failing to achieve your goals or living up to your expectations. It can also indicate that you can't overcome certain challenges alone.

Seeing Yourself Falling

If you are the one falling into your dream, you feel rejected, anxious, insecure, overwhelmed, inferior, helpless, and out of control. Seeing someone pushing you off a cliff means that you feel insecure in your life. You suffer from low self-esteem if you trip and fall from a cliff. In all contexts, you do not feel in control of your life. Falling from a plane while wearing a parachute indicates freedom and letting go of whatever is holding you back.

Tripping and Falling

If you can't see what you tripped over, it means someone in your life is getting on your nerves. If you trip on a banana or any other object, you need to take care of yourself and the people in your life. The dream can also have a positive meaning, like getting an unexpected and happy surprise.

Flying

Flying can be a pleasant or terrifying dream, depending on the context. It can mean feeling free and that everything is possible. You can go anywhere, do anything, and be anyone. It shows you can handle anything life throws your way.

The negative meaning behind this dream reflects that there is something in your life you cannot live with and are trying to escape from. Sometimes, this dream means you are stressed in your waking life.

Flying a Plane

Flying in your dream symbolizes that you are in control of your life and where you are heading. Planes take you from one destination to another, so the dream can indicate that you are going to another place or starting a new chapter in your life. If the plane crashes or you experience turbulence, you will face obstacles on your way.

Falling Down

If you are flying and suddenly see yourself falling, it means you're struggling with personal growth and self-improvement. You can have obstacles in your life that prevent you from advancing, and you need to overcome them.

Fear of Flying

Feeling afraid while flying suggests you are a negative thinker. These thoughts are preventing you from enjoying your life and everything it has to offer. It can also mean that you're attached to your past, have a need to always be in control, or your goals are hard to achieve.

Flying High

Flying high in your dream represents freedom, lack of obstacles, and success. You have overcome some challenges in your waking life, like getting a promotion you worked hard for or achieving financial success. However, this dream can also have a different meaning. You can constantly brag about yourself in front of others, and your subconscious tells you to be more down to earth.

Flying with Wings

If you dream that you have wings and fly like a bird, it indicates you are free-spirited or experiencing new beginnings and feeling hopeful. It can also mean great opportunities are coming your way and will bring you joy and happiness. The dream can symbolize feeling empowered and strong. You have succeeded in getting rid of everything that holds you back, and you feel invincible.

Struggling to Fly

Dreaming that you are struggling to fly or unable to stay in the air for more than a few seconds suggests that something in your life is preventing you from improving or advancing. It is trying to tell you where the problem lies, so pay attention to the context of your dream; it can provide you with clues.

Laughing

Laughing is always pleasant, but just like anything in the dream world, it can have positive and negative meanings. If your laugh is natural and not hysterical, it means that you are happy and satisfied in your waking life. Laughing can also mean you're overwhelmed with tension and stress, and you need to take care of yourself and have fun. The dream also represents your satisfaction with your life. Most people wake up smiling when they are laughing in their dream.

Laughing and Crying

Dreaming that you are laughing and crying at the same time indicates confusion. You have probably experienced difficult situations in the last few months, feel sensitive, and struggle to cope. Whenever you try to stay positive, you find yourself pulled back into a circle of darkness and negativity. No one can help you but you.

Laughing Loudly

This dream means you enjoy being the center of attention. You want all eyes to be on you, and you always try to get a reaction from others. There is something about you that makes people enjoy your company and laugh wherever you are around. You desire to be liked, which drives you crazy when someone dislikes you.

Laughing Quietly

Laughing quietly in a dream reflects your patience. You are calm and poised, and do not let stress get to you. No matter what the situation, you never react with anger or aggression.

Someone Else Laughing

Dreaming of someone laughing means that you will have happy experiences soon. You may go on a vacation with your friends or a loved one, or you will celebrate good news soon. The dream can also foretell that something you're waiting for will finally happen, like getting married, having a baby, or getting a promotion.

Someone Laughing at You

Dreaming of someone laughing at you means that something in your life requires attention, and you should force yourself to handle the situation. It can also indicate that you have a strong personality. This dream can also be a warning that you are about to receive bad news or are surrounded by negative energy.

Uncontrollable Laughter

This dream reflects your out-of-control emotions. You easily lose your temper and react without thinking. It is telling you to stop overreacting to every situation and think before speaking.

Running

Running is one of the most recurring dreams. It is not usually a pleasant dream since you either escape from something or chase someone. Generally, running means escaping reality, personal growth, getting away from your problems, overcoming challenges, and, in some cases, experiencing joy. If you are running fast and hard, you should find a goal in your life to run toward.

Running slowly means you will struggle with achieving your goals in real life. You could also be running to avoid something or someone in your real life, like a work task, an exam, or relationship issues. When you are running from or toward something, you feel anxious or guilty about an issue in your waking life. Running without a purpose indicates worry and anxiety about your future or feeling trapped or struggling with making a decision.

Running Away from Someone

Dreaming that you are running away from someone or something means that you're trying to avoid or escape from your fears. You feel in danger or threatened, so you flee. Sometimes, you can be running from something inside of you, like your impulses or inner struggles. Seeing the face of the person or thing chasing you can give you an insight into what is troubling you.

Running for Exercise

Dreaming that you are running for exercise represents working to improve yourself and your life. However, the dream can also indicate that you're wasting your effort on the wrong things, like a project or a career. Analyze and research the issue carefully before taking any steps.

Running in Fear

If you are running to save yourself from someone chasing you and are scared, you feel protected and safe in your surroundings. You can also be heading on a dangerous path, and this dream serves as a warning to have your guard up. This dream can also reflect certain issues you're struggling with in your waking life.

Running to Hide

If you dream you are running to hide, you should look at yourself and re-evaluate your life. You can be under a lot of stress and need to slow down, or things are changing around you, and you do not feel in control. This dream also symbolizes avoidance. There is an issue in your life you cannot confront, like a secret or a sad memory you're trying to block.

Running toward Someone

Running toward someone in your dreams has two meanings. It can indicate that you are working on a difficult goal but far from accomplishing it. In this case, evaluate your strategies to determine what needs change. It can also reflect your ambition and desire to achieve your goals immediately. You're on the right track, and you can achieve anything you set your mind to and turn your dream into a reality.

Unable to Run

Dreaming that you are trying to run but cannot move your feet is a recurring dream, usually resulting from REM paralysis. However, it can reflect that you're suffering from poor self-esteem.

In the land of dreams, nothing is as it seems. Drowning can have a positive meaning, while laughter can have a negative one. Pay attention to your dreams and understand the meaning behind everything you see. Your subconscious is painting you a picture, and every detail matters.

Chapter 4: Dream Locations and Meanings

Dreams take place in settings that are real or imaginary. More often than not, they change during the dream, while at other times, you do not even notice the location as the events take precedence. When people interpret their dreams, they are usually more focused on the scenario than where it occurred. However, similar to actions, your subconscious is also trying to tell you something through the location of your dreams.

Dreamworlds reflect your mindset. They don't symbolize a place but what you think of in your waking life. For instance, dreaming about your office means you're preoccupied with your job. If you dream about returning to school, you're concerned about the life lessons you hope to learn. Dreaming about your childhood home suggests you're still attached to the past. Once you understand the meaning behind different common locations, you will better understand yourself.

This chapter will cover different dream locations and the meanings and symbolism behind them.

Amusement Park

Dreaming of an amusement park symbolizes your need to take a break and have fun. Perhaps you have been working too hard and need more time for yourself. It can also indicate feeling nostalgic for your carefree childhood. The dream could further reflect your desire to escape reality, even temporarily.

Dreaming about an amusement park symbolizes the need for a break.
https://unsplash.com/photos/r6LQc9feEZQ

If you are not enjoying yourself in the park, you feel trapped and do not have any control over your life.

Crowded Amusement Park

Dreaming of a crowded amusement park reflects your fear of loneliness. You need the love and support of your family and friends to combat this feeling. It can also mean you are struggling with making a decision. Many people try to influence your opinion, and you cannot think clearly.

Roller Coaster

A roller coaster in dreams indicates that you don't take anything seriously. It means you are trying to better your life and take it one day at a time. Riding a roller coaster with a loved one symbolizes the highs and lows of your relationship. It represents your desire to have new and fun experiences with them. The roller coaster can also symbolize that your relationship with this person will change or external factors will impact both of you. These changes will be positive if you're having fun on the ride. However, if you feel scared or uncomfortable, they will be unpleasant. If you aren't enjoying the ride in the dream, you'll not embrace the changes in your waking life.

Beach

Seeing the beach in your dreams suggests reflecting on yourself and your life. You are about to undergo big changes that can be good or bad, like a marriage proposal or a breakup. It also means that you are at peace with whatever happens in your life. You have decided to look on the bright side and accept anything that happens to you with a smile and gratitude. This dream suggests you are about to go on a vacation that will be a much-needed escape so you can recharge and refocus on your goals.

Empty or Deserted Beach

This dream means you feel empty on the inside. Your subconscious is telling you to look inward to find yourself and fill the emptiness. Forget about what you have to do and focus on the things that bring you joy. This dream can also symbolize transition.

A deserted beach means you are exhausted and desperately need a break. You want to be in a place with nothing and no one to worry about but yourself.

Sunbathing on the Beach

This dream symbolizes nostalgia and returning to a time when you were carefree and at peace. It also means you long to experience something new and amazing.

Childhood Home

Dreaming about your childhood signifies feeling nostalgic for the past. You probably feel unsupported and unloved by the people in your life and are looking for the comfort of your childhood. Or simply, your brain is trying to escape the unpleasantness of your waking life to a safe and happy memory. It can also mean that you long for a time when life was simple. Sometimes, the past can bring bad memories and resentment, and your subconscious is telling you that it is time to confront it and let go of the anger and the pain.

Better Childhood Home

Dreaming of a better and bigger childhood home suggests that the principles and ideals you have grown up with have positively impacted your life. Your happy childhood has influenced the strong and successful person you have become.

Destroyed Childhood Home

Dreaming of your childhood home being destroyed suggests unpleasant memories are haunting you. It can also mean that an old secret you have kept all your life has now come to light. Perhaps you have created a false childhood image, and the truth is now being revealed.

Church or Temple

Seeing a place of worship in your dream, like a church or temple, indicates your need for support and guidance from a god or higher place. It also means two choices confront you, and you do not know which is right for you. You are also struggling with existential questions like "Why are you here?" or "What does the future hold?" Houses of worship in dreams can reflect your desire to connect with your spiritual side.

Being in a Church or Temple

If you are struggling with hardships in your waking life, this dream represents your frustration and confusion over what to do in this situation. You are desperate, feel there is no way out, and are about to give up on your goals. Your self-esteem is shaking, and you no longer have faith in your abilities. The houses of worship symbolize your faith. Being in a church or temple in your dream is a sign that you can overcome these obstacles.

Closed Church or Temple

Seeing a closed church or temple in your dream means you feel helpless and alone. Perhaps a close friend or a family member has recently disappointed you. Your subconscious is telling you to take the high road and open your heart to forgiveness.

City

A city in dreams symbolizes a fast-paced and lively lifestyle. It can indicate that your life is changing at a pace you are uncomfortable with, and you struggle with keeping up and should pause and reflect. Since the city is associated with new opportunities, this dream suggests you are hopeful and believe good things are coming your way. Dreaming of working in a city means your job is your number one priority, and it has impacted your relationships with your loved ones. Or you are unsatisfied with your current career and are looking for a change.

Abandoned City

An abandoned city in dreams suggests separation and the end of a relationship. Perhaps you are trying to save your marriage only to realize you are the only one holding on and the other person is no longer interested. This dream is a sign that you should walk away before you start resenting them. Or you will have a huge fight with a loved one that will escalate and end your relationship.

Wandering the City

This dream signifies your indecisive nature. You will struggle with making a choice soon because the two options will appeal to you. You do not want to make the wrong choice and regret it later. This dream is a warning that some people can take advantage of your confusion and influence you to make a choice that benefits them.

Dreaming you are wandering around a strange city suggests you will move to a new country or experience an unfamiliar situation. You will struggle with the change at first, especially if it involves meeting new people. However, in time, you will adapt and embrace your new life.

If you get lost while wandering around a city, it means you're struggling with making a decision related to your career. Perhaps you want to start your own business but are worried about taking the risk. It can also mean you got promoted in your waking life or were assigned a new project, and you feel overwhelmed by your new responsibilities. You find it hard to make any decision because you know it will impact other people. It can also indicate feeling confused in the workplace. Either management or your responsibilities have changed, and you aren't sure what is expected of you anymore.

Countryside

Dreaming about the countryside indicates feeling exhausted and stressed in your waking life. Your relationships and the people in your life can also make you feel constrained. Being in the countryside symbolizes the peace and freedom you crave. You desire to escape from your chaotic life to a quiet and natural environment. The dream further means that you feel free from the rules imposed by society.

Living in the Countryside

Dreaming of living in the countryside indicates that things will work out in your life. You have either found the person you want to spend the rest of your life with or finally found a career that makes you happy. You are finally in control of your life.

Visiting the Countryside

If you dream of visiting the countryside, you require a break or vacation to get away from it all. It can also indicate that you are about to experience positive changes in your life. Whatever is troubling you or causing you stress is about to end.

Forest

Dreaming of a forest may indicate feelings of insecurity.
https://pixabay.com/images/id-1072821/

Dreaming of a forest means you are looking for something that is no longer there. Walking in a forest can indicate feeling insecure and unsettled. It also symbolizes transformation and reflection. Your subconscious is telling you to look inward and reevaluate how you handle life's obstacles and find happiness. It can further mean that you should be aware of your surroundings to protect yourself to prevent problems.

Being in a Forest

Dreaming of being in a forest suggests that you should be cautious. You can have problems at work that require your full attention. It can also indicate that you will experience discord with other family members. This dream can serve as a warning that someone in your life will betray you. Do not share your fear or insecurities with people you don't trust; they can use your weaknesses against you.

Getting Lost in a Forest

This dream is a sign that you will probably experience disappointment and betrayal. It also means that you should be grateful for what you have because circumstances can change at any minute. If you are in a tough position right now, this dream is telling you to learn from the difficulties as they will make you stronger, and things will get better.

Library

Dreaming about a library symbolizes your vast knowledge and wisdom. Your loved ones often seek your advice and trust your opinion. It also indicates that certain information is hidden from you and that some people in your life are not what they seem. Your subconscious is telling you to do more research while being careful and alert to uncover what is hidden. This dream is further telling you to look within to find the answers you seek.

Empty and Abandoned Libraries

Dreaming of an empty library is a sign that you are about to face some trouble in your professional life. Your company may be facing financial problems and have to lay off some people, or your performance may not meet its standards, so you worry they may let you go. Perhaps, one of your co-workers will stab you in the back and cause you to lose your job.

Seeing an abandoned library in your dream implies giving up your professional and academic goals to focus on your family. Your subconscious is telling you to keep chasing your dreams, or you will live with regret.

People in a Library

Dreaming about strangers in a library means you should understand your strengths, weaknesses, and abilities before starting any new project.

If you dream about friends or family in a library and this person guides you, you are learning from them in your waking life. They will open your eyes to the knowledge you never even knew existed. If you are alone in a library, it is a sign that you will eventually achieve all your goals.

Long Hallway

Dreaming about a long hallway symbolizes your passion, leadership, enthusiasm, and courage. It also signifies transformation in your life. However, you are not willing to embrace the change. You want everything to stay the same. This dream further symbolizes nostalgia, worries, and insecurity.

Running Down a Long Hallway

This dream suggests poor health or sadness in your waking life. Your subconscious is telling you to slow down and focus on yourself. It indicates that something in your life requires your immediate attention. The dream reflects self-doubt. You do not believe you have what it takes to achieve your goals. It also implies you will experience the end of your business or relationship.

Walking in a Long Hallway

This dream suggests you are about to start a new chapter in your life and should be prepared for it. However, your subconscious is telling you to weigh all your options before making any decision.

Stairs

Stairs dreams signify personal growth and working to achieve your goals. They symbolize the steps you should take to be successful in your waking life. They also reflect the ups and downs you feel in your daily life.

Climbing up the Stairs

Dreaming you are climbing up the stairs symbolizes achieving your dreams. It reflects your ambitious nature. Long stairs mean your goal will not be easy to achieve, and you will face challenges along the way. If you're climbing the stairs with difficulty, you face setbacks in your waking life. Your subconscious may be warning you to pause and take care of yourself.

Going Down the Stairs

This dream signifies stepping down from a high position—like getting demoted at work. It also means that something in your life is stressing you out, and you feel crushed under its weight. Difficulty in climbing down the stairs symbolizes hesitation toward change. If you are easily climbing down the stairs, you are optimistic and confident about the future.

Tunnel

Dreaming about tunnels means you are ready to put the past behind you and focus on the future. They represent the road you take and the challenges you face in life. Tunnels reflect your strong abilities and positive attitude even when you face challenges and hardships. If you have this dream during a hard time in your waking life, your subconscious is sending you a message to stay strong and keep going. Knowing where the tunnel leads in your dream means you feel safe and secure about the path you are taking in your waking life. However, if the route is unclear, you feel uncertain about your choices.

Being in a Tunnel

This dream implies you have overcome challenges in your waking life that prevented you from achieving your goals. Now that you have accomplished them, you are about to go on a new and exciting journey.

Getting Stuck in a Tunnel

Dreaming about getting stuck in a tunnel suggests that a misunderstanding between you and a friend will lead to a huge fight. If the tunnel is dark, you are facing challenges in your life and looking for support. The darkness indicates you're feeling lonely. You're going through tough times and refuse to confide in or open up to anyone.

Every story takes place somewhere, and the stories in your dreams are no different. The location of your dream is a message from your subconscious about the state of your mind. Train yourself to notice where your dreams take place. The more locations you encounter, the more messages you must decipher. Understanding the meaning behind these places will give you an insight into your mind and reveal secrets about yourself that will surprise you. When it comes to interpreting dreams, follow the advice of real estate agents and focus on location, location, location.

Chapter 5: Dream Symbolism of the Four Elements

Symbols have been used throughout history to represent abstract concepts and feelings, and dreams are no exception. Dream symbolism in the four elements, fire, earth, water, and air, is an ancient Grecian technique of connecting with the natural world. In a dream, each element represents something unique. Whether you dream of a raging fire, a lush tropical beach, or a powerful gust of wind, the elements offer a unique way of understanding your innermost thoughts and feelings. This chapter will explore why understanding these elements' symbolism can help decipher the meaning of your dreams and gain a deeper insight into your subconscious.

The Four Elements

The origin of the four elements in dreams can be traced back to ancient Greece. This belief system, called the Four Elements Theory, was founded circa 450 BC and later taken up by Aristotle. It suggested that all matter on Earth was composed of four fundamental elements: Fire, water, earth, and air. According to ancient Greece, dreams were a manifestation of the four elements of the universe.

1. Fire was believed to be the element of creativity and passion
2. Water was associated with emotions and the unconscious
3. Earth was linked to physical reality

4. Air was connected to the spiritual realm

For the ancient Greeks, the four elements were essential to understand the human experience, and the dreaming process was an extension of this. This theory was integral to the development of Western philosophy and has been adopted by many cultures around the world. Today, the four elements are still used as an intrinsic aspect of dream interpretation.

- Fire is often seen in dreams as a symbol of passion, energy, strength, and creativity. It represents drive, ambition, and motivation. Fire can be a sign of a burning desire or a warning to be careful about something that could be dangerous.
- Earth is associated with stability, groundedness, and practicality. A reminder to stay in tune with the present moment and stay focused on what is important, earth represents your connection to the physical world and others.
- Water is an element of emotion, intuition, and creativity. It reflects your innermost feelings, as well as your subconscious desires. Water is also a sign of being open to change or learning from past experiences.
- Air is associated with communication, clarity, and freedom. A sign of needing to express yourself openly or being open to new ideas and perspectives, air represents a need for clarity in a difficult situation.

Let us take a deeper look into each of the four elements so you can assess the overall energy of your dream and get an in-depth insight into the dream's potential message and purpose.

Fire

Fire is a powerful symbol with a wide range of interpretations. From passion and transformation to destruction and anger, the symbolism of fire depends on the context of the dream, your feelings, and your current state of mind. A dream featuring a raging fire might symbolize:

- Intense emotions, such as anger, rage, or passion.
- A powerful transformation, such as a new beginning or a rebirth.
- Warmth, comfort, and security.

Fire can also be a symbol of destruction. If the dreamer is feeling overwhelmed or facing a difficult situation, fire may be warning them of danger ahead or represent the destruction that could happen if the dreamer is not careful. The color of the fire can be significant, too:
- Bright yellow or orange fire may represent energy, warmth, and passion.
- Red fire may symbolize anger or rage.
- Blue fire may represent a spiritual transformation or calming influence.

House Fire

Dreams about house fires are often interpreted as a sign of fear or anxiety. Fire symbolism is linked to insecurity, vulnerability, and anger, as well as indicating a lack of control and a deep-seated desire to take more charge of your life. The dream suggests:
- Lack of control.
- A situation that you feel powerless to change.
- A sign of destructive impulses or habits that you need to get rid of.
- Potential danger.
- That you are feeling overwhelmed.

Because fire is associated with transformation, destruction, and renewal, a house fire can symbolize:
- A desire to make a fresh start or a period of transition.
- Aspects of your life that need to be addressed or changed.
- Passion and intensity, so it could be representative of strong emotions.

Being Close to a Fire/Fire in the Distance

If you dream of being near a burning fire, it means you feel overwhelmed by intense emotions and need to find a way to express yourself.
- If you light the fire yourself in your dream, you strongly desire to create something new or start a new project. It also indicates that you need to take control of your life and be more assertive.
- On the other hand, if the fire in your dream is already lit, you feel energized and ready to take on new challenges.

Dreaming about a burning fire in the distance signifies an impending crisis or a warning of potential danger.
- If you are feeling conflicted or are struggling with something, the fire represents the intensity of the situation, and the distance represents how far away a solution feels.

A fire in the distance also symbolizes your passion and enthusiasm for something in your life, but you have yet to put in the work to achieve it. Nonetheless, your enthusiasm and passion burn brightly, and you are making progress toward achieving something.

You are on Fire

Dreaming about being on fire yourself is a sign of transformation and rebirth. This type of dream often indicates that you're going through a period of personal growth and development. It also signifies a desire to make changes in your life, such as changing careers or starting a new relationship, but you're afraid of failure or of being judged by others. Ultimately, the symbolism of this dream could be interpreted in different ways, depending on the context and the details of the dream. For example:
- If you dream of being engulfed in flames and feeling a sense of freedom, it means that you're ready to take risks and make bold changes in your life.
- Alternatively, if you feel overwhelmed by the flames, it is a sign that you're overwhelmed by life's challenges or feel stuck in an unsatisfying situation.

Someone Else is on Fire

Dreams about someone else being on fire could be a source of confusion and fear. It can be difficult to wrap your head around the symbolism of such a dream, especially if it involves someone you love. Whatever the case, remember that these dreams are symbolic and should not be taken at face value. Take the time to reflect on what the dreams mean and how they apply to you. In dream symbolism, someone else being on fire can indicate a need for change or transformation in your life:
- It is a sign of anger or resentment toward them and means that you must confront them and have an honest conversation.
- It is a sign of wishful thinking or a desire to see that person suffer in some way.

- It is a sign that you need to let go of something holding you back, whether it's a toxic relationship or a destructive habit

Essentially, dreams like this symbolize the end of a particular phase in your life or the start of something new and exciting. However, you must address whatever is holding you back before moving forward.

Earth

Generally, when you dream of earth, it symbolizes stability and security. Specifically, this indicates the need to stay grounded and connected to one's roots. It can remind one to stay true to oneself and one's values. Earth also represents:

- Fertility and growth, suggesting that the dreamer is in a good place in their life and can manifest their dreams and desires.
- A warning to focus on the present, as the dreamer's actions now will determine the future.
- A sign of abundance and prosperity, as the earth is abundant and always provides what is necessary.

The symbolism of earth in dreams is related to one's mother and family. It serves as a reminder that one must take care of family or cherish the time they have with them. As the earth is the ultimate nurturer, it represents the need for nurturing and compassion.

A Natural Disaster

Dreaming about natural disasters such as earthquakes, floods, hurricanes, and tornadoes can be interpreted in various ways, depending on the details of the dream. For example:

- If you dream of an earthquake, it represents an upheaval in your life. This could be something big, such as a move or a new job, or something smaller, such as the end of a relationship.
- Dreaming of a flood represents an emotional release. It symbolizes an overwhelming sense of emotions that you have been holding back.
- Alternatively, if you dream of seeing a flood, it is a sign of letting go of something holding you back, such as a toxic relationship or an unhealthy habit.
- Dreaming of a hurricane, tornado, or other powerful storm represents a period of intense growth or transformation. The

storm's intensity indicates the level of transformation that you are going through. If the storm was destructive, it means the end of an old chapter, while if it was calming, it means a new beginning is about to unfold.

Depending on how you felt during the dream, you can take these natural disaster scenarios as positive or negative. If you feel scared and helpless, it represents a lack of control over your life. On the other hand, if you feel energized and ready to face the danger, it represents a willingness to embrace new opportunities.

Being Buried

When you dream of being buried in the earth, it could mean a variety of different things depending on the context of the dream:

- A desire to escape from a difficult situation.
- Being overwhelmed.
- A desire to be protected from the outside world.
- The feeling of being stuck in life.
- A desire to be closer to nature.
- A feeling of being weighed down by the responsibilities of life.

When it comes to dream symbolism like this, consider the context of the dream and how you felt when you woke up. If you felt relief or a sense of liberation, the dream represents a desire to escape a difficult situation. If the dream left you feeling helpless or overwhelmed, it means you are overwhelmed. On the other hand, if the dream left you feeling safe and secure, it represents a desire to be protected from the outside world.

Seeing the Planets in the Sky

Dreams can be a fascinating and mysterious phenomenon. When you dream about seeing the planets in the sky, it can be a reflection of your innermost thoughts and emotions. These types of dreams symbolize:

- Ambition, exploration, and a desire to reach the stars.
- The need to expand your horizons and explore the world.
- A desire to better understand yourself and the world around you.
- Being overwhelmed by the enormity of life and the responsibilities that come with it. Your subconscious is telling

you to take a step back and reassess the direction in which you are heading.

Looking Down on Earth from Space

Dreaming of looking down on Earth from space is a powerful symbol of perspective and spiritual and physical distance. It represents understanding, clarity, and distance from your current situation. Your subconscious is telling you to look at a situation from a different angle, to take a step back, and gain some emotional distance. Seeing Earth from space represents:

- The need for spiritual growth and development.
- A reminder to take some time out of your busy life and spend it with yourself or nature.
- A sign to take a break from technology and reconnect with yourself and the natural world, allowing yourself to gain a new perspective.
- The need for physical distance or change.

Water

When you dream of water, it indicates an emotional state—feelings such as calmness, tranquility, balance, fear, anxiety, and turbulence. Water talks to the depths of your subconscious mind, which can be dark and mysterious, symbolizing feelings you cannot express in your waking life. Water also represents:

- Spiritual cleansing and renewal.
- A sign of awakening and spiritual growth.
- New beginnings and opportunities.
- A journey of transformation.

Finally, dreaming of water in any state implies a connection to the divine: A sign of being in tune with your higher self, which means you are ready to make positive changes.

The Ocean

Dreaming of the ocean may indicate emotional expressiveness.
https://www.pexels.com/photo/ocean-waves-1646311/

If you are swimming, sailing, or floating in the ocean, viewing it from afar or close up, this typically indicates that something is being released or washed away or that you're in the process of expressing yourself emotionally. It is also a sign of spiritual cleansing or a connection with the unknown. Because the ocean symbolizes the vastness of the unconscious and the inner depths of the soul, dreaming about it reminds you to trust your intuition and instincts and explore your depths. In some cases, dreaming about the ocean indicates a fear of the unknown or being overwhelmed by emotions or stress. Dreaming about the ocean represents:

- Growth and transformation.
- A new stage in life.
- A period of healing and renewal.
- A source of life and abundance in the near future.

Lakes and Rivers

Dreaming about lakes and rivers can be interpreted as a spiritual journey toward understanding yourself and finding your inner peace. More deeply, dreaming about lakes and rivers can represent transformation, renewal, and fertility. This is because their flowing nature

symbolizes the subconscious, the unknown, and the depths of our inner selves. Dreaming about lakes and rivers suggests:
- That you are searching for a deeper understanding of yourself.
- That you are looking to tap into your inner wisdom.
- A sign of creativity and inspiration.
- An association with emotional healing and the need to let go of the past.

Because the river and lake water represent the tears you may need to shed to move on from a difficult situation, dreaming about them means you need emotional release. They are a place of emotional safety and security for you to rest and heal.

Rain

Rain in dreams symbolizes cleansing and renewal, suggesting a time for change and new beginnings. If you feel like your life has been stagnant or dull, the rain in your dream shows that you need to shake things up and make a change. Or at least take a break and start fresh. In some cases, dreaming about rain indicates:
- Sadness and grief.
- An expression of your emotions and a sign that you need to take some time to process and heal.
- You need to take a step back and find a new perspective.
- You need to pay closer attention to your intuition and look for signs from the universe.
- You need to pay more attention to your feelings and trust your inner voice.

If you have been struggling with a project or problem, rain in your dream indicates success. It means your financial situation is about to improve, or your hard work will soon pay off.

Drowning

Dreams of drowning can be quite unsettling. However, it is a powerful reminder to pay attention to your feelings and take control of the situation. These feelings are related to the current state of your life or a particular problem or issue. When you dream that you're drowning, it means that you're feeling like you cannot keep your head above water. You may feel like you're stuck and do not know how to get out. This symbolism is closely related to feelings of being overwhelmed by a particular problem or the general chaos of life.

In some cases, it is a sign that you're trying to avoid facing a difficult situation or a problem you've been avoiding. The dream is telling you that you need to take control and deal with the issue to move forward.

Air

Air symbolizes freedom in dreams. As a symbol of liberation, creativity, and joy, if you dream of flying or soaring through the air, it is a sign that you are feeling emotional or spiritual freedom. Alternatively, dreams about air represent:

- Being overwhelmed.
- The need to take a mental or spiritual break.
- Communication, ideas, and thoughts.
- A connection with a higher power or your intuition.
- A sign that you need to open your mind to new ideas and possibilities.
- Spiritual understanding.

Suffocating

Dreams can be very mysterious, and interpreting them can be even more puzzling. However, dreaming of being suffocated has a very clear message: Your subconscious is trying to tell you that you are feeling overwhelmed by something in your waking life. Suffocating in a dream symbolizes feeling stifled by a situation or person or that you cannot make progress and express yourself in some area of your life. You ma feel trapped, whether it is in your job, a relationship, or a situation that you are unable to control. Dreams of this nature also mean:

- You feel your opinion or feelings are not being considered or respected.

These feelings of being overwhelmed can be quite daunting and could be the cause of your subconscious trying to express these feelings in your dream.

Feeling a Breeze

Dreaming about feeling a nice breeze is a sign of contentment and a symbol of a pleasant change coming your way. It also signifies a feeling of freedom, joy, and hope, as the wind is associated with liberation. A nice

breeze can represent:
- A new beginning, a new journey, or a fresh start.
- The presence of a spiritual guide or an angel watching over you and helping you on your journey.
- That you are about to experience a peaceful period in your life.

On a deeper level, dreaming about feeling a nice breeze signifies that something positive is coming your way. As a symbol of progress, success, and happiness, dreams like this mean you are moving in the right direction and are manifesting your dreams into reality.

Something Flying in Your Face

Dreaming about something flying in your face can be a scary experience, especially if it is one of those that jump scare you awake. But when they happen, they are a symbol of your fear of failure or fear of a certain situation in your life. Other meanings include:
- Something is coming your way that you are not prepared for.
- A situation that you're trying to avoid.
- You need to be more open and vulnerable in your life.
- You need to take a risk and be willing to face whatever comes your way.

Coming Up against a Storm, Flying Dirt, or Heavy Wind

Dreams about coming up against a storm, dirt, or heavy wind symbolize a chaotic situation in your waking life. Representing a situation in which you feel overwhelmed and out of control, dreams like this reflect stress and turmoil.
- A storm or wind is connected to the idea of change, a period of upheaval and rapid transformation.
- Dirt flying in your face is connected to new beginnings. A sign that you are ready to start fresh and make a new beginning.

Learning about dream symbolism of the four elements is an incredibly insightful and meaningful exercise. Each element—fire, earth, water, and air—holds a unique set of symbols and meanings. By understanding the symbolism of these four elements, you will get a deeper understanding of the hidden messages and meanings in your dreams. By uncovering your subconscious desires and fears and the deeper aspects of your life, you'll be on your way to a journey of self-discovery.

Chapter 6: Looking at Colors and Numbers

Dreams can be filled with strange symbols and images that initially seem nonsensical. Colors and numbers often appear and have special meanings. Colors associated with hidden emotions provide insights into your subconscious mind. Numbers, on the other hand, represent spiritual guidance and enlightenment. This chapter will explore the symbolism of colors and numbers in dream interpretation and how to use this analysis to unlock deeper meaning and gain insight into yourself.

Colors

When dreaming about colors, there is no single meaning or interpretation. Every person has a very personal experience and relationship with colors, so the explanation varies from person to person. However, in general, colors express emotions. They provide a framework for emotional insight and indicate a positive or negative outlook or feeling:

- Green symbolizes balance, harmony, growth, and fertility
- Blue signifies peace and tranquility
- Yellow symbolizes optimism and joy
- Red signifies anger, passion, or danger
- Black means sadness, grief, fear, and negativity

- White indicates a sense of purity, innocence, sterility, or emptiness
- Orange sky refers to optimism and enthusiasm

Colors that represent specific memories and events from your past:
- Vivid yellow symbolizes nostalgia for a certain time in your life

Color in dreams can be used to help you to understand your subconscious mind:
- Bright pink symbolizes a need for more love and nurturing in your life
- Deep green suggests a need for more inner balance and harmony

Ultimately, the meaning of colors in dreams is highly subjective and dependent on the individual. As you delve into the specifics of the following dream scenarios, consider the context of the dream, as well as how you feel during and after. Then, reflect on the recent events that have occurred in your life, as they may have influenced your dream in some way.

Black

Black is mysterious and powerful. It represents the unknown, shadows, and your subconscious. Often associated with strength and fortitude, black symbolizes protection, transformation, and strength.
- A dream in which everything appears in shades of black represents darkness and the unknown, suggesting a sense of fear.
- All black refers to a period of darkness before growth and light.
- If you are in a dark room, it represents disorientation and confusion.
- If the dream includes a black cat, it symbolizes bad luck or deception.
- Dreams of a black horse mean power and freedom.
- A black sky means death, either literal or metaphorical one, such as the death of an old habit or behavior.

Blue

Blue is the color of peace, tranquility, and deep understanding. Dreams with this color symbolize truth, faith, and communication and indicate that you feel emotionally calm and secure. Following that, blue

in a dream often represents a positive feeling or desire to find inner peace.
- A bright blue sky symbolizes a sense of freedom and openness.
- A soothing blue ocean represents calming emotions and a desire to stay grounded.
- Blue clothes, either yours or someone else's, symbolize security and protection.

Brown

Brown is a color of stability and practicality. It signifies organization, structure, and a connection to the natural world. Dreaming of brown can indicate a desire for something reliable. Essentially, you're looking for stability.
- A tree trunk symbolizes a need for grounding and stability.
- If you dream of a barren landscape, you are uninspired and lack motivation.
- Brown dirt on your hands refers to feeling lost. It means that you're feeling disoriented and need help finding your way.
- A brown suitcase symbolizes a journey.
- A brown car means success.
- A brown river represents the flow of life.
- A brown bird represents good luck or fortune.

Burgundy

Burgundy is a deep, rich color and symbolizes passion, ambition, and intensity. It represents courage, strength, and determination. Dreams featuring burgundy are often a sign that you are feeling empowered and motivated to take on a new challenge. In dreams, this appears as self-empowerment and strength:
- A burgundy dress symbolizes that you are taking control of your life or are about to embark on a new journey.
- If a car is burgundy, it means that you are driving your destiny and controlling where you are going.
- Walls of burgundy represent a barrier or protection from outside forces.
- A person in burgundy symbolizes that you are meeting a powerful and inspiring figure in your life.

Cream

Associated with innocence and purity, cream symbolizes a new beginning or fresh start. When cream is seen in a dream, it indicates a desire to be free from something or to start over. From a psychological perspective, cream is also associated with comfort and security, or the need for healing:

- A cream-colored blanket is a sign that you need to take time for yourself and relax.
- If you dream of a cream-colored wall, it's a sign that you feel trapped and need to find a way to break free.
- A cream-colored sky symbolizes peace and tranquility.

Gold

Gold is associated with wealth, power, and success. Indicating a desire for material possessions or a need for recognition or respect, gold means you have ambition, a drive for success, or a wish to be seen as important or valuable.

- A golden pot of coins means that you will soon become wealthy.
- A gold ring symbolizes commitment and long-term success.
- Other gold things in a dream can include golden statues, jewelry, and even clothing.

Regardless of its form, gold usually signifies something positive in your life.

Green

Green, the symbol of growth, fertility, and nature, indicates a hope for the future or a desire for abundance. When green appears in a dream, it is a sign that you are on the right path and need to trust your instincts and follow your dreams. Green has a calming effect, so it is no surprise that it appears in your dreams. From lush green meadows to emerald-colored lakes, green is a common sight in the dream world:

- A green tree symbolizes the growth of a relationship.
- A green field foretells an abundance of wealth and success.
- A ray of green light signifies hope.
- Green clothing is a sign of fertility or abundance.
- Green eyes symbolize intuition and knowledge.

Ivory

Ivory, the color of purity and innocence, symbolizes peace, tranquility, and balance. When ivory appears in a dream, it is a sign that you are in a place of security and comfort.

- If you see someone wearing an ivory gown, it symbolizes a need for spiritual purity.
- An ivory statue is a sign that you're ready to let go of something in the past and move on to something new.
- An ivory wall indicates that you're ready to build a new foundation in your life and create something fresh and exciting.

Lilac

The color lilac may indicate a dreamer's naivety.
https://www.pexels.com/photo/purple-wall-color-1293006/

Lilac is associated with joy and youthfulness. In a dream, this color represents the dreamer's innocence and naivety about a situation or person. It also signifies a need to break away from a situation and explore new opportunities. Dreams featuring things that are lilac can be quite telling as this color often has strong connotations:

- A lilac-colored sky indicates that you feel peaceful and content with the current state of your life.
- Lilac-colored flowers are a sign that you need more joy and beauty and are looking for ways to bring more of these into your life.

- A lilac-colored house means you seek a more harmonious and balanced home life.

Maroon

Maroon is often seen as a sign of power and authority. In a dream, this color represents the need to take control. It can signify a desire to be respected and admired. Dreams featuring things that are maroon can be interpreted as a sign of deep transformation, strength, and wisdom:

- A maroon sky indicates a dark period of your life.
- A maroon wall symbolizes a barrier preventing you from achieving your goals.
- Maroon clothing signifies a deep desire to be accepted or respected. It could also be a sign of feeling vulnerable.
- Maroon furniture is a sign of stagnation and lack of growth.

Maroon is also seen in dreams in the form of animals:

- A maroon snake indicates that you are facing a challenge you must overcome.
- A maroon bird represents transformation and freedom.

Mauve

Mauve is often associated with romance and tranquility. This color represents the need to find inner peace and relaxation in a dream. It also signifies a desire for meaningful connections. The color with a dreamy, mysterious vibe appears in dreams in many different forms. From a delicate mauve sunset to a deep mauve ocean, it signifies a range of emotions and feelings:

- A mauve sky represents peace and tranquility.
- On the other hand, a deep mauve ocean represents unease and even fear.

Orange

Orange is a sign of creativity and enthusiasm. In a dream, this color represents a desire for self-expression and the cultivation of ideas. It also signifies a desire to be more open and adventurous. Generally speaking, dreaming of orange things can be interpreted as a new opportunity or an exciting change on the horizon:

- A vivid orange sunset is a sign that you are about to embark on a new adventure.

- Orange flames represent a warning to take caution in some aspects of your life.

Peach

Peach is associated with contentment and happiness. In a dream, this color represents the need for balance and harmony. It also symbolizes a desire for stability and security. This warm, inviting hue can be interpreted in many ways, depending on the context of the dream and the person:

- For some, a peach-colored sky implies a sense of peace, calmness, and contentment.
- For others, if something usually white or gray is colored peach in a dream, it suggests something negative, like a warning against danger or a sign of illness.

Peach is also symbolic of fertility and abundance. For example, a person might dream of eating a peach and feeling full and satisfied.

Pink

Pink is seen as a sign of love and compassion. In a dream, this color represents the need to open up and show true feelings. It also refers to a desire for emotional closeness and intimacy.

- A pink teddy bear could be interpreted as a sign of comfort and security.
- Similarly, dreaming of a pink flower represents growth and rebirth.

On the other hand, pink is an indicator of something negative:

- A pink sky symbolizes a warning to the dreamer to be more cautious in the near future.
- A pink elephant represents anxiety or fear.

Red

Red is the color of passion, power, love, and anger. In dreams, it is a sign of intense emotions like fear or anger or the presence of a powerful force. A dream featuring lots of red can be a warning to take heed and pay attention to what is going on in your life.

- A red sky is a sign of danger and a warning to be careful.
- Red fruits symbolize the growth of new life.
- Blood represents death or the shedding of old ideas.

- A red rose symbolizes love and passion.
- A red stop sign symbolizes danger to come.

Silver

As the color of luxury, silver is associated with spiritual protection and the presence of divine guidance. It can be a sign that you are being held and supported even in times of difficulty.

- A silver moon refers to intuition and spiritual connection.
- A silver car is a sign of success.
- A silver ring symbolizes commitment.

White

White is the color of purity and innocence. In dreams, it represents new beginnings and a fresh start. It can be a sign of hope and optimism and that you have the power to make positive changes in your life.

- White doves are a sign of peace and protection.
- White clouds indicate a higher spiritual plane.
- White animals, such as horses or lions, represent strength and courage.
- White objects such as houses, castles, or furniture reflect the dreamer's home life, positively or negatively.

Yellow

The color yellow signifies joy, optimism, happiness, and good fortune. A sign of new beginnings and a bright future means you are ready to take on new opportunities and challenges.

- A yellow sky is a sign of hope.
- A yellow river symbolizes intense emotions.
- A yellow dress indicates a desire for change.
- Yellow shoes are a sign of adventure.
- A yellow car is a sign of luxury and good fortune to come.

Numbers

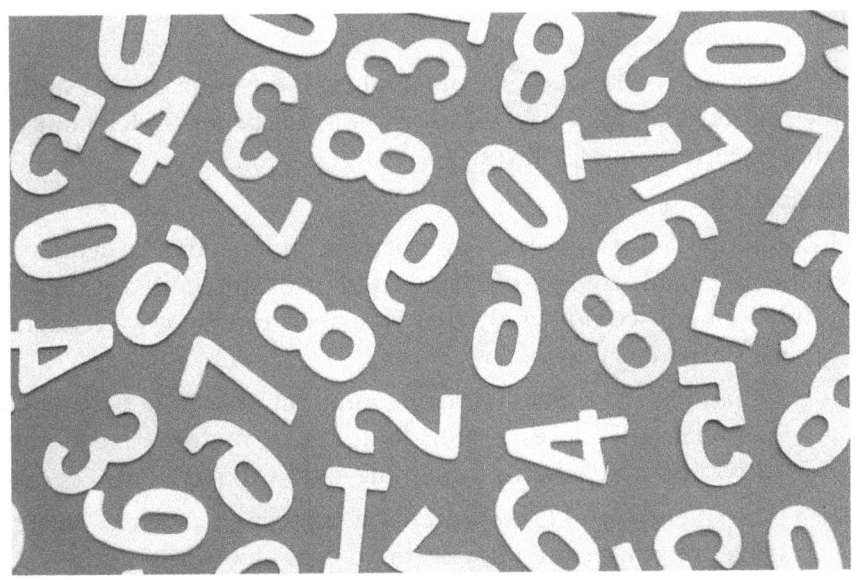

Numbers in a dream can represent many things.
https://www.pexels.com/photo/lots-of-numbers-1314543/

Dreams are a fascinating phenomenon, and they, more often than not, leave us wondering what they mean. Have you ever had a dream where numbers appeared? If so, you are not alone. Many people report dreaming about numbers. But what do these numbers mean? Numbers can represent:

- The passage of time, a countdown, a deadline, or a warning of sorts
- Your subconscious
- Guidance
- An area of your life that needs improvement

Specific digits mean something, too:

- The number three symbolizes creativity, growth, and expansion
- The number four represents stability and structure
- The number seven reflects spiritual understanding

Sometimes, numbers in dreams are literal. They could represent something significant in your life or act as a reminder of things you need to do:

- A phone number
- An address
- A bank account

Pay attention to the context and emotions of your dream and the specific number that appears. This way, you will better understand what your inner self is trying to tell you.

Number One

The number one symbolizes uniqueness, independence, leadership, self-confidence, and strength of character. For example, if you dream of the number one, it could signify that you need to take on a leadership role or take decisive action.

- Dreaming of a clock with the number one is a sign of great potential and success, often hinting that the time has come to take a risk and achieve something extraordinary.
- A sequence of 111 represents a trifecta of positive energy, a triplet of new beginnings, or the idea of a powerful trinity.

Number Two

A symbol of partnership and balance, dreams with the number two suggest the need for collaboration and harmony. It means you need to look for a partner or collaborator to help you reach your goals.

- The number two, in any form, is associated with a financial situation, such as having two sources of income or a bank balance with two digits.

Number Three

A sign of creativity, imagination, growth, and spiritual development, dreaming about the number three is a sign that you need to embrace your creativity and tap into your spiritual side.

- A telephone number that contains the number three signifies you are on the verge of achieving a goal.
- A cloud formation with the number three signifies creativity and abundance.
- A random object with the number three signifies you are about to embark on a new journey.

Number Four

The number four typically symbolizes stability and structure. Representing the four pillars of life—physical, mental, emotional, and spiritual—a dream with the number four is telling you to focus on stability and work on your life's foundations. When the number four appears in your dream, it is related to something practical and significant:

- Seeing a telephone number with the number four indicates that someone needs to contact you urgently or has a secret they want to tell you.
- Dreaming of a calendar with the number four indicates a looming deadline or an event that should not be missed.

Number Five

The number five represents change. As a symbol of transition or transformation, a dream with the number five in it tells you to embrace change and be open to new experiences.

- Five clocks signify impending stress or a reminder to stay in control of your time.
- A five-dollar bill is a sign that you're seeking financial stability or are feeling financially secure.
- A pentagram (a five-pointed star) indicates the need to reconcile innermost feelings and emotions.
- Five doors suggest the need to explore different paths in life.
- Five candles represent the need to be more aware of the spiritual realm.
- Five sticks of dynamite indicate a need for a dramatic change or transformation in life.

Number Six

Often associated with harmony and balance, the number six represents stability, peace, and balance. A dream with the number six in it is telling you to focus on achieving harmony and balance in your life.

- Six objects, such as six chairs or books, signify a need for balance or stability.
- Six children suggest a desire to be surrounded by love and support.
- A six-leafed clover suggests that you have the luck of the Irish on your side.
- A six-sided die symbolizes a desire to take a gamble and risk something for a potential reward.

Number Seven

Lucky number seven. Dreams with this number can be interpreted as a sign of good luck and fortune coming your way.

- Seven birds are a sign of good luck and success coming your way.
- Seven stars in the sky represent spiritual enlightenment.
- Seven coins signify the need to be more mindful of your finances.

Number Eight

The number eight is also seen as a powerful and auspicious number in many cultures, and it can symbolize abundance and prosperity. Dreams of the number eight signify that you will have many resources at your disposal and are on the right path.

- Eight people could mean that you are surrounded by supportive, caring people in your life.
- Eight objects mean you're trying to achieve something or a reminder to stay focused on your goal.

Number Nine

Very telling, the number nine is a sign that you're on the brink of achieving something important. It could mean you're on the cusp of a breakthrough and should keep pushing forward.

- The number nine as a date means you are nearing the end of something that has been occupying your life for some time.
- The number nine on your clock is a powerful reminder that it is time to look forward and start afresh.

Learning about colors and numbers is an interesting and exciting experience. There is much to explore, from the symbolic meanings of colors to how numbers can be interpreted. For instance, the symbolic meaning of colors gives you tremendous insight into your subconscious. On the other hand, numbers can be used to explore a variety of energies, from the physical world to spiritual and metaphysical realms. Thus, learning about colors and numbers can be a great way to gain a better understanding of your inner workings.

Chapter 7: Dreams with Animals and Plants

Have you ever had a dream which involved animals or plants? Animals, primarily, and plants, secondarily, are common symbols that appear in dreams, and they can have a variety of meanings. This chapter will cover the extensive symbolic meaning of dreaming about animals and plants. It will explore why these symbols may appear in your dreamscapes, what kind of messages or insights they could offer you, and how to interpret them.

Animals in Dreams

Animals often appear in dreams as symbols giving us greater insight into the unconscious and spiritual realms. Different animals represent distinct aspects of yourself, such as power, intuition, aggression, innocence, flightiness, or wisdom. They also represent a specific trait or feeling you strive to learn or embody. Paying attention to the animals in your dreams can be valuable for personal growth and self-discovery.

The animal in your dream can be a clue to its meaning. Different species have different symbolic connotations; understanding them is key to interpreting your dream.

Lion

The lion is a powerful and majestic symbol of strength, courage, and leadership. In dreams, it depicts the power and self-confidence required in your daily life. Alternatively, it symbolizes feeling or being trapped in an uncomfortable situation. It represents a need to act or make decisions to progress.

The lion also symbolizes primal fear and instinct. It often represents a deep inner fear or anxiety you may struggle to overcome. In some cases, this can be a fear of the unknown or a fear of change.

The lion is further associated with royalty and nobility, a symbol of power, strength, and authority in many cultures. In dream interpretation, it can indicate the need to be more assertive or take on a leadership role in your life. It also represents a desire for recognition or admiration from others.

Cat

Cats are symbols of mystery, magic, playfulness, and independence. They represent your inner wildness and capacity for autonomy, resourcefulness, and survival. They additionally symbolize your ability to hide and protect yourself from the outside world.

In a dream, cats can be seen as a sign of protection and symbolize your spiritual connection to the world. They represent an independent spirit or the ability to care for yourself. They could also represent mystery, intuition, and the unknown.

Dreams about cats are often echoes of your internal emotions, feelings, and desires. It is a message to connect with your intuition and inner wisdom. Moreover, dreams of cats can be interpreted as signs of your hidden potential and intuition.

Dog

Dreams about dogs often symbolize loyalty, companionship, and protection. Depending on the type of dog in the dream, it can be a sign of faithfulness or even possessiveness. It could represent innocence and playfulness if you dream of a small dog like a poodle or terrier. If you are dreaming of larger dogs, such as a German shepherd, it can symbolize strength and courage. If the dog is barking in your dream, it could indicate your need to defend yourself against someone or something. It could also represent a warning about potential danger coming your way.

Horse

Dreams about horses symbolize power and energy. Horses have long been associated with strong emotions like passion and freedom. If the horse is wild, it can represent wild energy that needs to be tamed. If the horse is calm and content in your dream, this reflects your emotional state and how you deal with strong emotions.

Dreams about horses can also be interpreted as a desire for freedom or movement. The horse may represent a need for change and growth in your life. Alternatively, the dream could tell you that it is time to step out of your comfort zone and take risks to achieve success. Horses can also represent your ambition, desire for power, or need to control your destiny. If the horse appears galloping in your dream, you are feeling powerful and capable of achieving success.

Some believe that the dreams of horses can also be interpreted as a sign of good luck and fortune. If the horse appears strong and healthy, this may indicate a prosperous future. Alternatively, if the horse is weak or dying in your dream, this could mean that difficult times are ahead.

Dreaming of a white horse could be interpreted as a spiritual sign, representing your inner spirit or higher self. Such dreams suggest your need to embrace a spiritual journey to reach enlightenment. If the horse is black, this could indicate ambition and power. Overall, the meaning of a dream with horses depends on many variables, such as color, behavior, and the overall context of your dream.

Elephant

Elephants are seen as a sign of protection.
https://unsplash.com/photos/P7L5011nD5s?utm_source=unsplash&utm_medium=referral&utm_content=creditShareLink

In dream interpretation, elephants represent strength, power, wisdom, and luck. They can be seen as a sign of protection. Dreaming of an elephant indicates good luck and fortune coming your way soon. It also suggests that you should be prepared for hard work and difficulties coming up in your life. Elephants represent strength and courage, which could signify that you are ready to take on any challenge.

In some cultures, elephants represent fertility and abundance. Dreaming of an elephant could mean you are ready to start a new chapter and open yourself up to all the possibilities it will bring. If the elephant is big, it could symbolize that you have much to offer and a great capacity for growth.

Bear

Bears represent strength and potential for courage. They often symbolize protection, so dreaming of a bear could be interpreted as a sign of protection from something in your life. Bears can also signify your need to take on more responsibility or assert yourself within your relationships or family.

Raccoon

In dream interpretation, raccoons symbolize craftiness and cleverness. They indicate that you need to use your problem-solving and critical thinking skills to find a creative solution to an issue you may face. If a raccoon appears in your dream, it can represent your lack of security and uncertainty. It could also mean hiding something from others or protecting yourself from potential danger. On a more positive note, a raccoon in your dream signifies the importance of adapting to your environment and being flexible.

More generally, raccoons symbolize the need to look at a situation from multiple perspectives and use intuition to reach the right solution.

Each animal has its singular symbolism and meaning, so paying attention to the details in your dream is essential. Pay close attention to any animal in your dream, as it could have a special message just for you. To put the qualities of animals succinctly:

- **Lion:** Power, courage, and leadership
- **Tiger:** Strength and aggression
- **Dog:** Loyalty and protection
- **Elephant:** Wisdom, patience, and kindness
- **Mice:** Timidity and meekness

- **Butterfly:** Transformation and rebirth
- **Frogs:** Fearlessness in new things
- **Birds:** Reaching for greater heights
- **Hawk:** Visionary qualities and the ability to rise above
- **Owl:** Intuition, insight, and clairvoyance
- **Horse:** Strength, freedom, and the power to take control
- **Wolf:** Resourcefulness and instinctual power
- **Unicorn:** Magic, hope, and ability to transcend
- **Fish:** Intuition, creativity, and emotions
- **Reptiles (snakes or dragons):** Unknown fears and hidden truths

Dreams about Bugs

Bugs in dreams often represent feeling out of control, overwhelmed, or vulnerable. They symbolize a fear of the unknown or feeling insignificant in the grand scheme. Bugs often appear in dreams when you feel your life is spiraling out of control and you are struggling to keep up with all the changes around you.

Dreams about bugs signify the presence of a problem or issue that is causing you stress. It may also mean something in your life needs to be addressed or dealt with.

Ants

Dreams about ants signify hard work, determination, and perseverance in achieving your goals. Ants are often seen scurrying around in an organized manner, which can symbolize a need to get organized to achieve your goals. Ants can also represent industriousness, ambition, and productivity.

Spiders

Dreams about spiders often signify a need to look more closely at something in your life and ensure that you see it from all angles. Spiders can also represent your intuition and ability to sense danger, or they may be a warning of something being hidden from you.

If you dream of a spider crawling on your body, it may indicate someone is trying to take advantage of you. Alternatively, it could mean a part of your life you neglect, such as an unhealthy relationship or toxic habit. This dream may encourage you to look at this area and make changes.

Dreams of being trapped in a spider's web signify that you feel stuck in a particular situation or relationship. You may think that you cannot get out of the web, and no matter how hard you struggle, you cannot escape. This dream asks you to look within yourself and understand why you feel trapped before trying to change your life.

Bees

Dreams about bees indicate hard work, ambition, and productivity. They can signify your enthusiasm for projects or activities that you are working on. Bees represent the pollinating power of hard work and the importance of working together to accomplish tasks and projects. When you see a bee or swarm of bees in your dream, it is a sign that you are working hard to achieve something. It reminds you to focus on the task before you and strive to reach your goals.

Dreams with bees also symbolize that someone's negative energy is being directed at you and their attempts to disrupt your success. If you dream of a swarm of bees coming at you, it could indicate that someone is trying to interfere in your life or stop you from achieving your goals.

Fleas

Dreams about fleas often signify feeling overwhelmed and helpless in a certain situation. Fleas can also represent being irritated by someone or something but not having the power to do anything about it.

Cockroaches

Dreams about cockroaches often signify feeling powerless and helpless in the face of a problem. They can also symbolize feeling dirty and disgusting or having a physical or emotional issue that needs to be addressed.

Flies

Dreams about flies often represent feelings of being swamped and overwhelmed. They represent feeling powerless or unable to stop something from happening. Flies can be an annoyance in the dream, often indicating a feeling of being pestered or harassed by someone. In some cases, flies could represent a feeling of being a victim to someone or something. Alternatively, if the flies are orderly and not bothering you, it could be a sign of good luck.

Wasps

Dreams about wasps often represent difficult and uninviting situations. It could be a sign that you are feeling overwhelmed by a problem in your life or facing resistance from someone. Wasps can sometimes be a warning of danger or that something terrible is about to happen. They signify aggression, betrayal, or tension in your relationships.

Wasps can also be seen as a sign of pride or ego. You may find yourself feeling overly confident about your abilities or particularly ambitious. This is a message that you must take a step back and assess the situation before making significant decisions.

The context of the dream is also consequential; for example, a lion might have different meanings depending on whether it is in a zoo or attacking you. In the former case, it could mean your strength is being caged in or restricted somehow. It might signify a need to confront your inner demons in the latter. Similarly, the location of the dream is also important. If you dream about a large, powerful animal in an open field, it could symbolize freedom and the power to take control of your life. On the other hand, if it is in a dark and narrow cave, it could represent feeling trapped and suppressed.

The number of animals can be telling as well. One animal in a dream could represent the self, while two or more could symbolize the various aspects of your personality and how they interact.

Another factor to consider is the animal's behavior. Is it friendly or hostile? Passive or aggressive? Tame or wild? An animal's behavior in a dream offers insight into your current mindset and attitude. For example, if you dream of a tiger peacefully lounging in the sun, this could indicate that you feel relaxed and content in your current situation. On the other hand, if you dream of a tiger snarling and attacking you, this may mean that something or someone is threatening you.

Dreaming of a fight between two animals can signify an internal struggle or conflict within ourselves. It could also represent two parts of your life that oppose each other and must be reconciled. Animals in harmony could indicate a sense of peace and balance within yourself.

In addition to the species and behavior of the animal, it is essential to consider the dreamer's personal history and relationship with that particular type of animal. For example, if a dreamer had a traumatic experience with a specific animal, that could play out in their dream. This is incredibly influential if the dreamer feels fear or intense emotion upon seeing the animal in their dream.

Dreams with animals provide a unique insight into the subconscious, as they often represent aspects of yourself that you may not have been aware of or had difficulty expressing. Animals in dreams can symbolize instinctive behavior, primal and untamed emotions, or the power to tap into your deepest desires. Paying attention to the animal's context, behavior, and personal history can help you better understand your inner self and the forces that shape your life.

Dreams about Plants

Dreams about plants and trees can also be highly symbolic, as they are often strongly associated with growth, life, fertility, and a connection to nature. They can represent the health of a relationship, your physical well-being, or signify spiritual transformation. In dreams, plants symbolize various emotions and experiences, from birth to death and growth to decay.

The type of plant that appears in your dream is essential, as each species has unique meanings. For example, dreaming of a lush and vibrant garden could represent abundance. On the other hand, if the plants are wilted or dead, this could indicate that something is lacking or stagnating.

Trees

Trees are potent symbols of growth, life, and nature. A dream featuring a tree suggests that a person is ready to move forward and reach for success. Trees also represent knowledge, growth, and stability that can help overcome difficult times.

Dreams of trees can also relate to one's personal life and symbolize a solid or close relationship with others. Trees can represent family members, friends, or even higher power. In dreams, trees may also be interpreted as symbols of fertility and abundance.

Some trees have deep spiritual and religious connotations, such as the Tree of Life from Christianity or the Bodhi Tree from Buddhism.

Cactus

Dreams of cacti can be associated with protection, independence, and power. Cacti also symbolize strength in the face of adversity. They can indicate that someone is struggling to cope with a problematic situation or survive a challenging period. Cacti dreams suggest that the dreamer is feeling isolated and alone.

Coconut Palm

Coconut palms are usually associated with knowledge, wisdom, and progress. In many cultures, the coconut palm is considered a symbol of abundance, fertility, and growth. Symbolically, they represent a sense of resilience and strength, as they can grow in even the most adverse conditions. In dream interpretations, dreaming of a coconut palm could signify transformation and progress. It represents spiritual growth, new beginnings, changes in your life, and increased knowledge.

White Birch Trees

White birch trees often represent good luck, success, and hope in dreams. They symbolize flexibility, resilience, strength, and overcoming obstacles. These trees represent the need to be more flexible in life and to stay focused on the goal despite any difficulties that may come your way.

White Oak

White Oak is a beautiful and majestic tree representing courage, strength, and longevity. This tree suggests perseverance, stability, and a sense of security in dreams. It is a symbol of good luck and long-term success, so if you see a White Oak in your dream, it could represent a positive and encouraging outlook.

White Oak is also associated with the will to overcome obstacles and take on new challenges. If you dream of a White Oak, it can remind you to have faith and remain strong in difficult times. This tree also represents wisdom, patience, and fertility.

Dreams of Flowers

Flowers are often viewed as symbols of beauty, purity, and love in dreams. Dreaming of flowers represents the start of something new or a blossoming of ideas and thoughts. A bouquet can symbolize the gathering of courage, love, and strength that you need in life. A single flower can be a sign of innocence and vulnerability or even a reminder to care for yourself.

Rose

Roses are perhaps the most popular flowers in the world and often represent love, beauty, strength, innocence, and joy. In dreams, roses can symbolize various things; they often represent your feelings in your waking lives. For instance, if you dream of red roses, they may express passionate love, while white roses in your dream can signify purity and innocence.

Lily

The lily is a symbol of innocence, beauty, and purity. In dreams, it represents a sense of peace, serenity, and a longing for something beautiful. Dreaming of a white lily symbolizes purity and innocence, while a yellow lily may signify a desire for joy and happiness.

Sunflower

The sunflower symbolizes joy, creativity, strength, and growth. Such dreams often represent these qualities and signify hope and positivity. It indicates that you are headed in the right direction and can achieve your goals. It is also a sign of faith and optimism, as the sunflower always turns its face to the sun. Sunflower dreams often signify that you are entering a season of prosperity and abundance.

Morning Glory

Morning glory dreams are believed to be connected with new beginnings and fresh starts. It can symbolize the start of a new journey in life or a new project. Dreaming of these flowers often represents the potential for growth, fertility, and a strong connection to nature. They are also associated with the ability to heal oneself and others.

Tulip

Tulips are a sign of creativity and freedom.
https://unsplash.com/photos/Z-6bfsa6rD8?utm_source=unsplash&utm_medium=referral&utm_content=creditShareLink

Tulips are a popular and beautiful flower known for their bright colors, long stems, and simple petals. In dream interpretation, tulips are seen as a sign of beauty, freedom, and creativity. They often show up when you need to express yourself or open up to new ideas. When you dream of a tulip, it may signify that you need to look at things with fresh eyes and find inspiration in something new.

Plants and animals are common habitants of your dreamscape, and they often appear in symbolic form to give you important messages about your waking life. In addition to general symbolism, each type of plant or animal can have a special meaning when it appears in your dream. Taking the time to examine and interpret these symbols can be a helpful tool for understanding your subconscious and gaining insight into your life. However, remember that dream interpretation is personal, and the meaning of these animals and plants differs from person to person. It is best to explore the symbolism of a dream in the context of your own life and experiences.

Chapter 8: Dreams about Body Parts

Dreams are an incredible yet intricate phenomenon that holds an infinite array of symbolism and meanings. Dreams containing body parts, in particular, can be especially confusing as they can have many different connotations and layers of interpretations. While some may represent things like physical health or developmental growth, others refer to feelings and emotions within yourself or interactions with those around you. Inevitably, unlocking the true meaning behind these dreams can sometimes be a difficult task. This chapter sheds light on the confusion of dreams about body parts. Through exploring the symbolism, one can better understand why their dream is present and what it is trying to tell them about their life and current situation.

Hair

Hair is a common dream symbol, and the meaning changes depending on its context. Dreaming of styled hair might represent vanity, while a haircut in a dream could symbolize a new start or phase in your life. Unruly or chaotic hair often reflects feeling overwhelmed and out of control, while clean and neat hair indicates feelings of contentment and stability. Generally, long hair is associated with femininity and youthfulness, while short hair suggests strength and maturity. Hair can also mean spiritual or creative energy when seen intertwined with vines or other natural elements; this type of dream may suggest you need to express yourself creatively or re-establish a connection to nature.

Head

Dreams involving the head tend to symbolize your intellectual ability and how you process the events in your life. For example, a dream about having a large head could symbolize feeling "headstrong" and thinking you know better than anyone else. In contrast, if you dream of having a small head, it could mean you're overly humble or feel inadequate. Dreams about an injured or diseased head can symbolize mental distress or an inability to process your current reality. These dream symbols provide insight into your subconscious mind and offer valuable clues about yourself.

Brain

Dreams about brains often symbolize your power of thought and intellect. They are a sign that your mind is trying to process and contain a large amount of information. The symbolism can have a range of themes depending on the context; if a dream involves emotions, for example, it might suggest that the dreamer is subconsciously working through feelings or conflicts within themselves. Alternatively, if the dream mainly revolved around problem-solving tasks, it could indicate the dreamer is feeling pressure to find solutions to life dilemmas. Thus, when dreaming about brains, consider the other symbols associated with their presence to interpret the real deep-seated meaning of such dreams.

Nose

Dream symbolism of the nose reflects a "sense" you have for a certain situation—which can take many forms. For example, if you dream that someone has a large, prominent nose, it could signify they are aware of what is happening around them. On the flip side, dreaming of an absent or non-existent nose can suggest someone is not paying attention to their environment or trying to avoid responsibility. It's also been said that the size of the nose in your dream could correspond to how much effort you're putting into something—with a larger, more prominent nose representing more effort than a smaller one.

Teeth

Teeth are a common symbol dreamt of by people all over the world, with various interpretations as to what they mean. Dreams involving teeth often symbolize anxieties and fears, representing how these fears feel; sharp and painful. Teeth can represent power or control; if someone is portrayed as having vicious, razor-sharp teeth, it could represent fear of that person's influence. One could also dream about budding teeth in childhood, representing growing mental responsibilities with age. These teeth might even foreshadow future successes or failures in life. Alongside this, teeth represent communication, or having issues with your teeth in dreams can mean you're having difficulty making yourself heard or getting your message across. If a person has to have their teeth treated in the dreamscape, it can signify overpowering emotions that need tending to. Ultimately, dreaming about teeth can have numerous meanings depending on the context, so paying attention to details while interpreting such dreams is important.

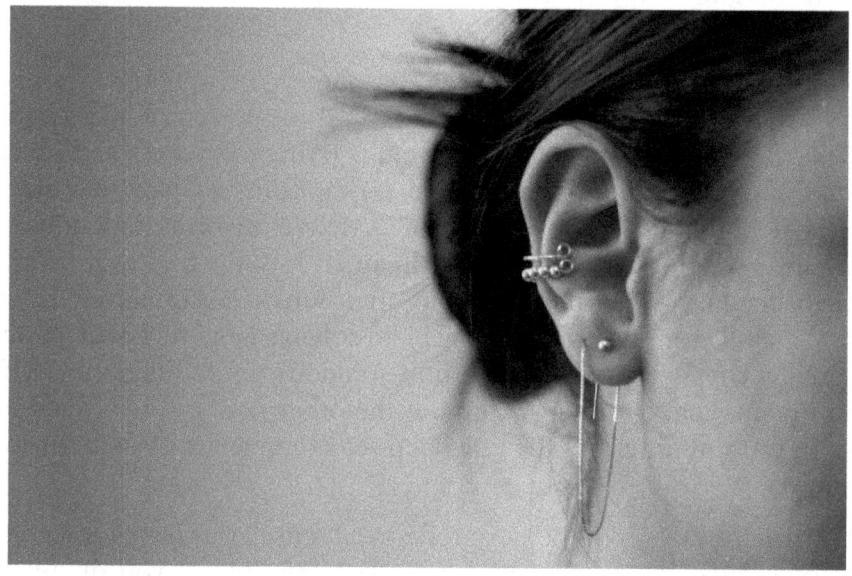

Ears have different meanings in a dream depending on the context.
https://unsplash.com/photos/AVJ321HJFl4?utm_source=unsplash&utm_medium=referral&utm_content=creditShareLink

Dreaming about ears can mean various things depending on the context. From spiritual to physical senses, dreaming of ears indicates that you are listening to something or someone. Ears in a dream often represent a person's ability to trust and be trusted. Symbols of objective perception, ears can suggest that an individual is paying attention, seeking knowledge, and being open-minded. In some cases, dreaming of ears also signifies obstacles blocking communication with others and deceit from someone close to you or even yourself. For example, if your ear is blocked or clogged, it may mean inner turmoil, or you're overwhelmed with thoughts and opinions that do not align with your beliefs. Ultimately, dreaming about ears conveys the overall of listening carefully with intention and discernment.

Back

Dreams featuring backs signify the different layers of protection and support you have in your life. A back symbolizes strength and security, so a dream about having a strong and solid back can represent emotional stability and a newfound belief in your trustworthiness. On the other hand, if you dream of having an injured or weak back, this may signify feelings of vulnerability or insecurity. Additionally, a dream about someone else's back can suggest that you're over-reliant on them for safety and comfort, which may be negatively impacting your emotional well-being. More broadly, dreams featuring backs suggest something hidden or something hidden within you that needs protecting, and you need to strengthen those areas before moving forward in your life.

Tongue

Dreams involving tongues can have many meanings; however, they generally relate to communication or miscommunication. A dream where you are speaking with an uncontrollable tongue might symbolize feelings that the speaker is not being heard, while dreaming of someone else's tongue could represent the feeling that the dreamer is completely outside of a conversation. Likewise, seeing an abnormally long tongue can indicate having difficulty conveying your thoughts to others. Saying something with a tongue made up of food could show dissatisfaction and suggest your words are not being taken seriously. An unmovable tongue might reveal feeling powerless and unable to express opinions, warn others, or simply be heard by those around you. All these can be seen as indications of anxiety around communication.

Breasts

One of the most common dream symbols, breasts are often associated with nourishment, femininity, and fertility. The symbolism of breasts can indicate a need for comfort and nurture in waking life in both males and females. Breasts may carry overtones related to maternal protection when viewed as a nurturing entity, while the sexuality of breasts can also be represented in dreams to symbolize lustful desires or a sense of connectedness. In general, dreaming of breasts represents physical or emotional nourishment, deeply embedded spiritual connections, and the possibility of motherhood. While these are some core ideas around breast symbolism, each dreamer's experience will ultimately be based on personal interpretation determined by current life circumstances.

Nipples

Dreaming about nipples may indicate that you seek ways to connect with another person, either intimately or generally. It could also symbolize a desire for nourishment and comfort and a search for emotional sustenance. Additionally, dreaming of nipples forms part of sexual themes as they are connected to one's most intimate parts, where feelings of desire are produced and explored in dream-states. By understanding the different concepts connected with dreaming of nipples, people can understand their unconscious desires better and get new insights into their lives.

Arms

Arms represent strength, power, aggression, and protection. Sometimes dreams of arms represent feelings of being armed with abilities or resources to handle life's tasks and challenges. They may symbolize the ability to reach out for help or for someone to reach out and offer assistance. Other times, dreams about arms may indicate a need for self-defense or an effort to defend a loved one against danger.

Abdomen

Abdomen dream symbolism is quite fascinating and has a multitude of meanings. Generally, the abdomen is associated with self-control, emotions, financial stability, and issues of fertility or infertility. When dreaming about your abdomen, it could indicate that something you have inside you needs attention and release. It could be a reminder to focus on maintaining balance in your life and controlling any extreme emotions that may be ruling your behavior. Alternatively, it could symbolize the structure of one's identity or a need for financial freedom to feel secure. Abdominal pain or wounds in the dream world can indicate infertility issues, while sculpted abs can represent strength and power. Dream symbols about the abdomen are powerful indicators that healing needs to occur to restore harmony in one's life.

Fingers

Dreaming about fingers has a lot of symbolism, depending on context. Generally, fingers represent assertiveness and strength. However, if the fingers in your dream are broken or mutilated, this may represent feelings of helplessness. If you find yourself counting your fingers in the dream-state, this could suggest that you are feeling overwhelmed by daily responsibilities and tasks. Dreaming of shaking hands with someone else can often signify a connection between two parties—it generally represents understanding and respect for each other's opinions. On the other hand, if you're clenching your fist in the dream, you might feel angry or frustrated—and perhaps you lack control over something occurring in your life. Understanding different symbolic fingers can reveal what is happening in your mind and is quite fascinating.

Palm

If a dream features a person holding their right palm open toward you, it is often interpreted as a sign of reconciliation or friendship. When featured in dreamscapes with loved ones, clutching someone's hand could represent their comforting presence and protection against life's difficulties. Seeing the palm of your hand in a dream often symbolizes hope or trust that you are beginning to have in yourself—like having faith to find the courage to start something new or overcome obstacles. It could also be a reminder that you possess the strength to confront fearful situations or take on ambitious endeavors. Consequently, dreams featuring palms of hands can mean many things, from protectiveness to hope—a universal symbol with various themes and interpretations.

Genitals

Dreams involving genitals are surprisingly common and can often carry deep psychological messages. Generally, having genital dreams means the dreamer is transitioning in some way, exploring a new identity, or embracing an existing one. It may also signify the opportunity to make a powerful shift in perspective, allowing you to take ownership of your life. For some people, it represents a sexual desire or the integration of their gender identity. Additionally, dreams that focus on genitals can symbolize how someone experiences themselves on the most intimate level, highlighting both positive and negative elements of their self-image. Overall, dreams featuring your sexual organs provide insight into how you navigate power dynamics within yourself and in your relationships.

Buttocks

The buttocks are a prominent dream symbol representing sensuality, fertility, and physical power. Dreams often reflect the need for dreamers to express themselves or move freely. This can be interpreted as a search for passion and independence from external expectations. The buttocks have also been linked to growth and exploration in different aspects of life, such as career goals, relationships, and self-reflection. Symbolically, the buttocks may suggest that you are working toward coming into your own power and embracing yourself fully.

Ankles

Ankles have long been a symbol with several different layers of meaning. In some cultures, ankles represent stability and home—feeling secure and rooted in your life. A dream in which ankles are prominent may represent a need to focus on making plans or forming strong foundations for yourself. Ankles can stand for sensuality and femininity. A dream involving ankle-bearing clothes could reveal that you are exploring your sex appeal, while ankle imagery around heights may suggest being held back by feelings of self-doubt or insecurity about the future. While the symbolism for ankles varies from culture to culture, it is undeniable that these flexible joints conjure up powerful emotions—both positive and negative—no matter where you come from.

Knees

Dreaming about knees is a particularly unique and fascinating topic. The symbolic meanings behind knee-related dreams vary greatly depending on what appears in the dream. Generally, dreaming about knees represents flexibility, vulnerability, or stability. For example, if a person's knees are strong and stable in the dreamscape, this could symbolize self-confidence and resilience. Alternatively, if the knees appear weak and fragile in the dream, it can suggest feelings of instability or weakening resolve regarding an issue or situation. Similarly, if a person can move their body parts with ease in the dream—from bending down to crouching—this may allude to one's level of flexibility in life or your ability to think outside of the box quickly and effectively. Altogether, these interpretations are valuable insights for interpreting knee symbolism within dreams.

Legs

Dreams, filled with symbolism, can uncover your subconscious thoughts and emotions, so the meaning of some bizarre elements may have particular significance. One commonly experienced dream symbol is legs. Generally, dreaming about legs can represent your desire for stability and balance or indicate how you approach a certain situation by either walking away from it or stepping forward. It may also point to feeling bound or restricted in life, struggling to move ahead, or trapped without an escape. In addition, dreams about legs may imply confidence and strength or symbolize overcoming obstacles regardless of size.

Alternatively, dreaming about arachnoid legs could symbolize difficult moments that will soon pass if you remain resourceful. Leg dreams are often highly individualized and can depend on the feelings the dreamer associates with them to get an accurate interpretation—so think carefully before coming to any conclusions.

Toes

Dreaming about toes can be puzzling, but it actually says quite a lot about your current state of mind and emotions. Toes often symbolize balance in your life; if your toes are healthy and you can walk without difficulty, it may mean that you are feeling balanced in every aspect of your life or that you're feeling hopeful. However, if the toes appear broken or unhealthy, it likely means someone is feeling out of control. Additionally, dreaming about any type of movement involving toes, such as running or dancing, could represent joy and happiness, while dreaming about step-counting suggests focusing on details or avoiding trouble. Overall, the dream symbolism of toes ranges from feelings of accomplishment to hopelessness, depending on the dreamer's current situation.

Blood

Blood is a powerful symbol that has been used to represent a variety of themes throughout history and across cultures. Historically, it has often been associated with life and death and pain or suffering—reflecting its position between the two states. It can also represent intense emotions like anger, violence, and passion. In dream symbolism, blood may be interpreted differently depending on the context in which it appears. Sometimes it may signify loss or sadness, but it can also signal protection or healing. On an even deeper level, blood in a dream might point toward ancestral memory, soul loss, and even spiritual transformation. Whatever form its presence takes, blood dreams are thought to have unique significance as they often reflect intense internal struggles of one's subconscious nature.

Bones

Bones are a common symbol in dreams, representing both life and death. Dreams featuring bones can often represent something that has died or a cycle that has been broken, such as the breaking of an old habit or attitude. On the other hand, they can symbolize strength, resilience, and ancestors who have passed on their wisdom and knowledge. For example, dreaming of an old ancient skeleton may represent a connection to your past and how it influences your life today. Additionally, dreaming of multiple or incomplete bones may indicate a feeling of being incomplete on some level, with certain areas of your life needing attention. All in all, bones are powerful symbols filled with deep meaning that capture the fragility and beauty of life.

Chapter 9: When Supernatural Beings Appear

Your subconscious generates dreams. This part of your mind is responsible for imagination, intuition, and hidden desires and values. Besides images of yourself and regular beings, your imagination can also create supernatural characters or beings. Dragons, angels, spirits, sprites, and dwarves are just some of the common characters that might appear in people's dreams. This chapter explores the meaning of these supernatural characters appearing in dreams, analyzing the symbolism and variations.

Dreams about Angels

Dreaming of angels is a positive sign. Angels can offer wisdom, protection, guidance, assurance, and purification. In many cultures, angels are also considered messengers of the gods; however, they can have other functions, too. Some angels specialize in specific spiritual matters, and they will provide their assistance in that field. Guardian angels have a powerful connection to their charge and stay with them for most of their lives. Other angels simply materialize because they were available at that time and noticed their help was required.

Whichever type of angel appears in your dreams, they'll likely come in the same way each time. They can appear on a sign, fly, talk, or sing to your dream reality. Angels can also emerge in more subtly forms, including:

- Rainbows in the sky
- Other angelic symbols in the sky
- White feathers around you
- Feeling nurturing energy around you
- A sudden flash of light
- A voice that seemingly comes from nowhere
- The feeling of an invisible hand touching you
- Tingling sensation on your body or head

If an angel appears in your dreams (whether in person or through symbols) and you notice that you're feeling happy when you wake up, you have been blessed with their energy. It could also signify that you've needed reassurance for an upcoming challenge or advice for overcoming toxic influences.

If an angel is singing or talking to you in your dreams, they're opening your soul for their wisdom. It helps to share your grievances and worries so they can understand you better. This dream symbolizes your triumph over a past hurt or upcoming challenge. It can act as a form of intervention—in case you know that you need reassurance or advice. Whether the angel's words sound familiar to you or not, do not worry. They carry an eternal blessing your soul will understand and embrace without words. If you remember an angel talking to you but cannot recall their words, try to bring them back in bits and pieces through meditation. Your conversation will likely be stored in your subconscious. You just need the right tool to access it. When you do, you'll know in which direction to move forward.

Angels and demons often appear together and interact in dreams. If you see them fighting, this indicates that you're experiencing an inner conflict. It's most likely about right or wrong decisions or heading in the right direction. Maybe something is holding you back from moving toward a better path. This hindrance can be represented by the two opposing forces in your dream. The inner struggle can also stem from negative emotions, addictions, powerful urges, or similar self-limiting behavior.

The dreams will go away after acknowledging your conflict, focusing on surrounding yourself with good energies, and fighting off the toxic influences that cause the dispute. If they don't, you still have issues to work through.

If you dream of angel wings, you're protected by a powerful energy. If you focus hard enough, you'll feel this energy surrounding you. This dream will likely appear when you're going through a challenging period and need added protection.

While grown angels appear prevalently in dreams, some people also dream of baby angels of cherubs. If you notice an innocent-looking baby angel suddenly appear in your dreams, you're being offered extensive protection from above. These beings have many heavenly roles, including protecting the entrance to the Garden of Eden, which speaks of their closeness with God and the other angels. If you dream of a baby angel, you'll face a sudden major hurdle in life and need any angelic help you can get to overcome your challenges.

Dreams about Demons

Demons in dreams are never a good sign. These beings are linked to hostile forces. If they appear in your dreams, you have every reason to be alarmed. You are likely being affected by negative energies in your waking life. These energies can have detrimental consequences for your life. It could be an unpleasant work situation or relationship with a boss or colleague, bringing you down and blocking your professional development. Or, it can represent a place where you would feel safe but have to spend many hours—resulting in anxiety and other imbalances between the different parts of your life. Demons can also be linked to complex real-life individuals who secretly want you to fail. These complex individuals hide their true (demonic) face very well. You must be careful about interacting with such people to reveal who they are.

Dreams about Dragons

Dreaming about dragons has several meanings. The particular circumstances, the color and shape of the dragon, and their behavior all affect the meaning of this dream. In ancient Western cultures, dragons were often viewed as adversaries that warriors needed to defeat to secure their community. Because of this, many view "dream dragons" as harbingers of problems, destruction, and suffering in real life. Angry dragons also denote negative sentiments and behavior, typically born of anger and loss of control.

That said, in Eastern cultures, dragons have a very different image. They are thought to bring good luck, protection, and balance into people's lives. If you dream of a magnificent, colorful wingless dragon that acts friendly, it could be that you're yearning for freedom and balance. If it's a recurring dream, you're on your way to establishing this balance.

Dragons in dreams can symbolize power, authority figures, or your desire to have these characteristics. Dragons are also known to be eccentric. Dreaming about them can indicate that you have a passionate personality and are prone to finding unorthodox solutions for your problems. Or, you may have a hidden desire to express your passion, seek out new adventures, or regret missing opportunities to have funds in the past.

While dreaming about angry dragons can be scary, remember that these creatures often hint at your pent-up subconscious emotions and repressed thoughts. It can further imply an issue or conflict with another person in your work or personal life.

Dreams about Dwarves

If you see a dwarf in your dream, you are lucky. These unusual creatures are symbols of good fortune and surprises. It could mean you will win the lottery and have enough money not to worry about your finances for a while. Or, you might receive an inheritance or an unexpectedly good return on investment. If there are several dwarves in your dreams and you know that you'll be playing the lottery, this suggests that you should share your ticket with others so that they can take part in your good luck.

Dreams about Spirits

Dream images of spirits are probably the most common in dreams of supernatural beings. Nearly all ancient cultures have myths and records about spirits. Knowing this, it is not surprising that these creatures made their way into the imagination responsible for dream aspects. Most cultures agree that spirits can be ambivalent in nature. They can appear as visions, voices, or symbols in dreams, providing guidance, healing, and protection or, in some cases, causing disruption.

The meanings of spirit dreams can vary depending on the circumstances and actions of these entities in the dream world. Some believe that vivid dreams about spirits—particularly the spirit of your loved ones—indicate a strong connection and the actual appearance of the soul in your dreams. Dreaming about fictional spirits is just your brain's way of processing information related to your thoughts and emotions.

In most cases, dreaming of spirits indicates that you have unfinished business in your waking life. This association stems from the common belief that spirits that come back to visit also have unresolved issues in this world. Besides this, spirit dreams can denote uncertainty and uncoordinated thought processes. You may be at a crossroads in life and unsure where to go next. Or, maybe you're just curious about where life leads you but cannot help feeling nervous about it. Due to their ethereal nature, dreaming about spirits may be about you feeling invisible in your personal or professional life.

Spirits in dreams are a comforting phenomenon because they represent life after death. However, they can be seen as signs of mortality. For example, if you aren't taking care of yourself, dreaming about spirits can be a warning that you should start paying more attention to your health.

Spirits can also be seen as reflections of your hidden side, the part you aren't comfortable with and don't want to confront. For example, if you dream about a spirit you can't see, just feel and notice the signs they're sending you. Consider doing some introspection to see what you're trying to hide about yourself. There might be something you pretend not to see, but your subconscious will still sense it.

Spirits rarely speak to you directly in your dreams, but they might do other things. If the spirits in your dreams are moving items around you, this could indicate that you lack control of some areas of your waking life.

The appearance of spirits in your dream can be a stressful experience. If you feel haunted by the spirit or suffocated by its negative energy, this indicates that you feel overwhelmed by people or situations in the real world. You might also fear the unknown, so you stick to familiar waters, even if this hinders your progress and growth. If you're someone who often worries about the future, you're likely to have this dream. No matter how insignificant the event is, you can't help but expect the worst possible outcome. Constantly thinking that something untoward will happen soon will make you worried and project your thoughts and emotions into your subconscious. Haunting spirits further signify a vulnerable emotional state. If you feel negative about someone or something in your waking life, now is the time to deal with them so that you can regain control of your feelings.

If you dream about being a ghost, it could mean that you are experiencing extreme guilt about past events. Maybe you've hurt someone intentionally and never had the chance to say sorry or rectify the situation. Confronting your guilt can help you overcome it. Some people also have a paralyzing fear of spirits in their dreams. Again, this is fear from real life projected into your dream world. You'll need to look around for its cause and overcome your fear by taking a more positive approach to the situation.

If you dream about the spirits of loved ones who have passed away, the dream is about your connection with them. You might need to have a final talk with them to find closure. They might need reassurance that everything will be all right and that you've accepted their passing and moved on with your life.

Dreams about Sprites

Dreaming about sprites reflects your hope and confidence in your abilities to reach your goals. Just like angels, fairies in dreams are also good omens. Fairies usually seem like friendly creatures, so dreaming about them is associated with happiness. You may earn a significant achievement in life or obtain something you have desperately missed or thought impossible to achieve. Or, you may have found an item or connection you have lost.

While dreams about sprites rarely have negative connotations, you should still be careful. There are malicious fairies that are anything but friendly and helpful. If you dream of a mischievous fairy, this indicates that your emotional life is out of balance. If you feel scared of the spirits in your dreams, this could signify that you have issues in one of your relationships. Maybe someone wants to be a part of your life, even if you do not wish to have any connections with them.

Dreaming of a fairy wand is a message full of wisdom. It often means that you should listen to people around you when making important decisions, as they will have some wise suggestions. This particularly applies if you want to make a profit on something. Sprites can give you plenty of financial gains—you'll just have to listen to their advice.

Vampires in dreams symbolize your energy being drained in waking life.
https://www.pexels.com/photo/a-woman-dressed-as-a-vampire-14395497/

Dreams about Vampires

Vampires are known to feed on the blood of living people. If they appear in your dreams, it could mean that something or someone is draining your energy in your waking life. Blood symbolizes the energy that sustains your mind, body, and soul—something you cannot survive without. Dreaming about vampires is a warning for you to look closely at your environment and identify which parts are sucking the life out of you. Think about the areas of your life in which you have difficulty moving forward, or feel that you are not doing a good enough job. Maybe your employer is setting unreasonable deadlines for your projects, causing you to fail to finish them. Or, you might have a controlling partner who does not let you express your personality and needs in your relationships. You can just as well have a friend constantly complaining about something, bringing you down with their negativity and taking your time away from more productive pursuits.

Spirit Guides

Most spirit guides are souls residing in the spiritual realm. Instead of moving on to another life cycle, they have chosen to remain and watch over their living descendants. These are the souls of the ancestors, recently passed loved ones or pets, or people you've looked up to during their life. However, spirit guides can also be supernatural beings, including fairies, angels, and demons.

You are paired with a spirit guide who can best serve you in any situation. This can mean that you will have several spirit guides at a time. For example, if you're in a tough situation, you may need the complementary strengths and wisdom of an ancestor and an angel. The ancestor will provide you with the knowledge you need to find a solution, while the angel will empower you with their guidance.

Your spirit guides know you better than you know yourself, which makes them helpful in spiritual growth and healing. This is also why they will not appear in the form you would expect them to. Most people are unaware of their spirit guides being around because they appear in unique forms—like patterns in a dream, for example. If you see a character trying to guide you through your dreams, this is a common sign of a spiritual companion being at work. They may point to a specific place in the dream world, tell you to follow them, or show you a symbol representing the next step you need to take.

Some guides only appear for a short time, help you through a particularly difficult time, and then leave once your issues have been resolved. Let's say you have had a recurring dream about a supernatural being, but it stopped. This could have been a spiritual companion that has fulfilled their purpose. Other guides are there to assist you in your relationship, experiences, business deals, or events; however, when these end, the entities will move on, too.

Other companions are like experts in their field (like archangels) and appear and disappear as needed. Some guides are just there to help you overcome your loss. For example, if you dream about a pet you've lost recently, it might be their soul telling you that it's time to move on. Most people have one or more lifetime guises. You meet these souls in childhood, and they'll stay with you for the rest of your life. They appear in dreams, visions, and symbols in your environment. They help you uncover your gifts, guide you toward the right path, and help you stay on your chosen path. Spiritual companions can take the shape of any animal, plant, or supernatural being. If you have recurrent dreams about a specific supernatural entity, animal, or plant, this could be your spirit guide's way of trying to establish contact. Your guides can be persistent, especially when they know you need them. There are many reasons why your spirit guides will not appear in their original form. For example, many people cannot handle seeing a spiritual guide's true face. If your guardian thinks you aren't ready, they'll only send you subtle signals and appear in other forms until you've bonded with them and are ready to accept their true nature. Different entities have different abilities. Your spirit guide might not appear in front of you in your dreams because they simply can't.

Chapter 10: Advanced Dream Interpretation Techniques

Dreams can be filled with strange, mysterious characters and symbols that seem to have no real-world equivalent. They are a reflection of the subconscious mind, and as such, they can reveal hidden thoughts, emotions, and desires that you may be unaware of in your waking life. However, dreams can be difficult to understand, as they are filled with symbols that can seem confusing or meaningless. While some people believe that dreams have a universal meaning that can be easily deciphered, the truth is that the interpretation of dreams is a highly personal and subjective process.

One of the limitations of dream interpretation is the idea that there is a universal meaning behind dream symbols. For instance, some people believe that a dream about a snake always represents danger or temptation; however, the truth is that the interpretation of a dream symbol is unique to the dreamer. In fact, the same symbol can have different meanings for different people, depending on their personal associations and cultural background.

This chapter focuses on the importance of personal associations, emotions, and context in dream analysis. By exploring how you feel during the dream, focusing on the characters and objects that stand out to you, and considering the context of the dream, you can gain a deeper understanding of what your dream may be trying to tell you.

Asking the Right Questions

Recalling a dream can be a daunting task, especially if the dream seems fragmented or confusing. Fortunately, by using the 5Ws technique, you can start to piece together the details of your dream and make sense of what happened. Once you have a basic understanding of the details of your dream, it is time to use the answers to guide the interpretation process.

Who were the characters in your dream, and what roles did they play? What objects or symbols stood out to you, and why? Where did the dream take place, and what was the significance of the location? When did the dream occur, and what events led up to it? By answering these questions, you can start to uncover the hidden messages and meanings in your dream.

It's also important to explore any significant events, emotions, or thoughts from the previous day that may have influenced your dream. Dreams are often a reflection of your subconscious thoughts and emotions, so it's possible that something from your waking life may have triggered the dream. Perhaps you had a stressful day at work, or maybe you had an important conversation with a loved one. As you work through the interpretation process, pay close attention to your emotions and feelings during the dream. Did you feel scared, anxious, or overwhelmed? Or did you feel happy, loved, or content? The emotions you experience during the dream can offer important clues to the underlying messages and meanings.

Here is an example you can consider for learning how to interpret your dreams better:

Let's say that you dreamt you were at a party with your friends. Here's how you could use the 5Ws to analyze the dream:

- **Who?** Who was at the party with you? Were they people you know in real life, or were they strangers?
- **What?** What happened at the party? Did you have fun, or did something go wrong? Were there any objects or symbols that stood out to you?
- **When?** When did the dream occur? Was it during the day or at night? Did anything happen before the dream that might have influenced it?

- **Where?** Where was the party held? Was it a familiar location or somewhere new?
- **Why?** Why were you at the party? Did you have a specific goal or objective, or were you just there to have fun?

Let's say that upon reflection, you realize the people at the party were your high school friends who you haven't seen in years. You had a great time at the party, but you remember feeling a bit out of place. You also noticed that there was a clock on the wall that kept ticking faster and faster. Using this information, you can start to explore the underlying messages and meanings in your dream. Perhaps the dream represents a desire to reconnect with old friends but also a fear of feeling out of place or not fitting in. The ticking clock could symbolize a sense of urgency or the feeling that time is running out. Alternatively, it could represent a fear of missing out on opportunities or not making the most of your time.

By exploring these ideas and paying attention to your emotions during the dream, you can start to uncover the hidden messages and meanings in your dream and gain a deeper understanding of yourself and your subconscious mind.

Emotions are important to consider when interpreting dreams.
https://unsplash.com/photos/_VkwiVNCNfo?utm_source=unsplash&utm_medium=referral&utm_content=creditShareLink

Examining Emotions and Feelings

Emotions are a crucial element to consider when it comes to dreaming interpretation. Dreams often tap into your deepest feelings and emotions—how you feel during the dream and when you wake can give some important insights into what the dream might be trying to tell you. So, you must consider your emotions during the dream to analyze them effectively. Were you feeling anxious, scared, or overwhelmed? Or were you feeling calm, joyful, or curious? These emotions can offer significant clues as to the meaning of the dream. For example, feeling afraid of a character in the dream may indicate a sense of vulnerability or insecurity, while feeling comforted by that same character might indicate a need for support or guidance. When you woke up, did you feel relieved to wake up from a scary dream? Or did you feel sad to leave a pleasant dream behind? These emotions can provide further insights into the underlying messages and meanings of the dream.

When interpreting dream symbols or characters, consider the emotions associated with them. For example, a dream about a snake might evoke feelings of fear or disgust for some people, while others might feel fascinated or intrigued. These emotional responses can influence how the snake is interpreted in the dream. Similarly, a dream about a loved one may have very different meanings depending on whether the dreamer felt happy, sad, or conflicted in the dream. Emotions can offer important clues as to what the dream is trying to communicate and help you unlock hidden messages and meanings. Consider these examples to understand how emotions play into the interpretation of a dream:

- **A dream about flying:** If the dreamer feels joyful and free while flying, this could symbolize a sense of liberation or the ability to rise above challenges in their waking life. However, if the dreamer feels anxious or scared while flying, this could symbolize a fear of failure or loss of control.
- **A dream about water:** If the dreamer feels calm and peaceful while swimming in a body of water, this could symbolize emotional balance and tranquility. However, if the dreamer feels overwhelmed or anxious while navigating choppy waters, this could indicate a sense of being overwhelmed by emotions or life's challenges.

- **A dream about a house:** If the dreamer feels happy and comfortable in the house, this could symbolize a sense of security and belonging. However, if the dreamer feels uneasy or scared while exploring the house, this could indicate a fear of the unknown or feeling lost in their waking life.
- **A dream about a loved one:** If the dreamer feels happy and loved while interacting with a loved one in the dream, this could symbolize a deep connection and sense of support. However, if the dreamer feels conflicted or upset while interacting with the loved one, this could indicate unresolved issues or a need for closure.
- **A dream about a car:** If the dreamer feels in control and confident while driving a car, this could symbolize independence and self-determination. However, if the dreamer feels out of control or anxious while driving the car, this could indicate a fear of losing control or a need for guidance in their waking life.

Using Creative Interpretation Techniques

By approaching dream analysis with an open mind and a willingness to explore different perspectives, you can uncover hidden symbols, associations, and connections that might not be immediately apparent. Creative interpretation techniques involve thinking outside the box and considering multiple possibilities for what a symbol or character might represent. They encourage you to trust your instincts and draw upon your experiences and personal associations when interpreting your dreams. In the following sections, several advanced dream analysis techniques will be explored.

1. Amplification

This technique involves expanding on the images and symbols in your dream by exploring their historical, cultural, and personal associations. It involves exploring the rich web of associations and meanings surrounding a dream symbol or image. This technique is based on the idea that a dream image can have many layers of meaning and that by delving deeper into these meanings, you can better understand the message behind the dream.

To use the amplification technique, you start by identifying a symbol or image that stood out to you in the dream. Then consider all the possible meanings and associations that come to mind when you think of that symbol. This could involve drawing on personal experiences, cultural symbols, historical references, and other sources of inspiration. By exploring these associations and amplifying the symbol's meaning, you can uncover new insights into the dream and its significance.

For example, let's say you had a dream about a cat. Using the amplification technique, you can start by considering all of the possible meanings and associations of a cat. Consider the cat's physical characteristics, such as agility, independence, and grace. Also, consider cultural associations with cats, such as their role in ancient Egyptian mythology as protectors of the afterlife. Finally, reflect on your experiences with cats, including any positive or negative emotions you associate with these animals. You may realize that the cat symbolizes your desire for independence and freedom or represents a sense of mystery and intrigue in your waking life.

2. Active Imagination

An active imagination is a powerful dream analysis technique involving engaging with your dream's symbols and images through visualization and active participation. With an active imagination, you do not just observe your dream images; you immerse yourself in them and explore their full range of meanings and associations. To use active imagination, start by identifying a symbol or image that stood out to you in your dream. Then, try to visualize yourself interacting with that symbol or image, using all your senses to immerse yourself into the dream world fully. Imagine yourself talking to a dream character, exploring a dream landscape, or participating in a dream event.

Let's say you had a dream in which you were walking through a dark alleyway. You felt scared and vulnerable in the dream, and shadowy figures lurked in the corners. When you woke up, you still felt a sense of fear and unease, and you were not sure what the dream might be trying to tell you. To use active imagination to analyze this dream, you might start by visualizing yourself back in the dream, walking through the alleyway once again. As you walk, try to pay attention to the details of your environment: What do you see, hear, and feel? Are there any particular sensations or emotions that stand out to you?

Next, you could try to interact with the dream environment in some way. For example, you might try to find a way out of the alleyway or confront the shadowy figures lurking there. As you interact with the dream, pay attention to how your emotions and thoughts are changing. Do you feel more or less afraid? Are you experiencing any sense of empowerment or control? As you continue to engage with the dream in your visualization, you may uncover new insights and associations. For example, you may realize that the dream represents a fear or anxiety you have been struggling with in your waking life. Or, you might discover that the dream is pointing you toward a situation or relationship that feels unsafe or threatening.

3. Dialogue

The dialogue technique is a powerful tool for dream interpretation, as it allows you to explore the relationships and interactions between different elements of your dream in a more nuanced and dynamic way. Rather than simply analyzing each element independently, you can use dialogue to create a more complex and layered understanding of the dream as a whole. To use the dialogue technique, start by identifying two or more elements of your dream that seem to be in conflict or conversation with each other.

Let's say you have a dream in which you are standing on a beach, looking out at the ocean. As you watch the waves, you notice a small boat in the distance heading toward you. As the boat gets closer, you see it is piloted by a figure you cannot quite make out. As the boat pulls up to the shore, you realize that the pilot is actually your father, who passed away several years ago. He invites you onto the boat and begins to steer it out into the open ocean. As you're sailing together, you feel a mix of emotions—excitement, joy, and a sense of deep sadness at the same time.

To use the dialogue technique to interpret this dream, imagine a conversation between yourself and your father on the boat. What would you say to him, and what would he say to you? What emotions would you express, and how would he respond? As you imagine this dialogue, you will uncover new insights and associations about your relationship with your father and your emotions and desires. For example, you might realize that the dream is tapping into your longing for connection and intimacy with your father or that the boat represents a journey or transition you're currently going through.

4. Gestalt

The Gestalt technique is another great tool for dream interpretation to help you uncover deeper insights into the patterns and themes that underlie your dreams. To use this technique, you will need to approach your dream with an open mind and a willingness to explore its various elements and relationships. For example, let's say that you dream of walking through a crowded marketplace, browsing the stalls, and chatting with vendors. As you're walking, you notice a recurring pattern of red and green colors, which seem to appear in different forms throughout the dream—from the fruit and vegetables at the stalls to the clothing of the people around you.

To use the Gestalt technique to interpret this dream, try to look at the dream as a whole and explore the relationships and connections between the different elements. What do the red and green colors represent to you, and how do they relate to the other elements of the dream? What patterns and themes emerge when you look at the dream as a whole? You might realize that the red and green colors represent different sides of your emotional life—with red representing passion and intensity and green representing growth and abundance. Or you might see the crowded marketplace as a symbol of your desire for connection and social interaction, and the recurring colors highlight the different emotional experiences you encounter in these situations.

These advanced interpretation techniques can help you better understand your dreams and uncover hidden messages and meanings that you might have missed with a more basic analysis. However, keep in mind that dream interpretation is subjective, and there is no one "right" way to interpret a dream. The key is to stay open-minded, explore different possibilities, and trust your intuition. Do not be afraid to experiment with different approaches and techniques until you find what works best. Trust your intuition and allow yourself to be guided by your insights and inner wisdom.

Glossary of Dream Symbols

Colors

Black: Black suggests feelings of sadness or despair in a dream; however, it can also reflect power and strength. It may further represent obstacles that need to be overcome.

Blue: Blues are usually associated with feelings of peace and tranquility in dreams. They may also signify spiritual guidance or positive communication.

Brown: Brown points to feelings of stability, reliability, and comfort. It can also indicate a need to be grounded in reality.

Gold: Gold generally symbolizes wealth and riches in dreams but can also represent wisdom and spiritual growth.

Gray: Gray is typically associated with neutrality in dreams. It may suggest a lack of emotion or feeling or an impending decision on which one has yet to make up their mind.

Green: Green generally represents balance, harmony, and growth. It can symbolize renewal, fertility, or prosperity.

Orange: Orange often relates to creativity and indicates abundant energy and enthusiasm.

Pink: Pink represents love, romance, and femininity. It could also symbolize compassion and understanding.

Purple: Purple typically symbolizes mystery, spiritual awareness, or higher understanding in dreams. It can also suggest a connection to the supernatural.

Rainbow: Rainbows are often associated with hope and joy but can also signify transformation or good luck. They may represent an inner need for balance and harmony.

Red: Red can symbolize strong emotions such as love, anger, passion, and intensity. It can also represent danger or warning.

Silver: Silver typically indicates spiritual strength and inner wisdom. It can also reflect the ability to see through deception or lies.

White: White is often seen as a sign of purity and peace in dreams. It could be indicative of new beginnings and clarity of thought.

Yellow: Yellow is typically associated with joy, happiness, optimism, and good luck. It could also represent intelligence and mental clarity.

Animals

Bear: Bears represent power, authority, and leadership skills. If one appears in your dream, it could be time for you to take charge of a situation and make decisions.

Bee: Bees represent hard work, diligence, and productivity. If one appears in your dream, it may be time for you to put in more effort to reach success.

Bird: Birds represent freedom and spiritual growth. They may suggest that you take risks and make changes in your life to grow and succeed.

Butterfly: Butterflies often symbolize transformation and new beginnings. Dreaming of a butterfly could suggest you are ready to leave the past behind and embark on a new journey.

Cat: Cats often symbolize independence, grace, femininity, and mystery. They can also indicate that you are ready to explore new ideas or opportunities.

Deer: Deer typically represent grace, gentleness, and sensitivity. If one appears in your dream, it may be time for you to approach a situation with more care and understanding.

Dog: Dogs represent loyalty, protection, and devotion. Dreaming of a dog could mean it is time to put more trust in the people around you or seek help from them when needed.

Dragon: Dragons represent power, strength, and courage. Dreaming of a dragon may suggest it is time to draw upon these qualities within yourself to succeed.

Elephant: Elephants represent wisdom, strength, and patience. They may suggest you take a step back and assess your situation to move forward.

Fish: Fish in dreams often represent creativity, fertility, abundance, and luck. They could suggest that you take advantage of an opportunity presented before you.

Fox: Foxes symbolize intelligence and cunningness. Dreaming of a fox may suggest it is time to use your wit and knowledge to get ahead.

Horse: Horses represent power, strength, and endurance. They can also signify progress on your journey to reach your goals.

Lion: Lions are symbols of courage, strength, and confidence. They can also suggest that you need to be more assertive to get what you want out of life.

Monkey: Monkeys usually symbolize mischievousness and playfulness. Dreaming of a monkey may urge you to relax and have fun while pursuing your goals.

Owl: Owls are often associated with mystery, secrets, wisdom, and intuition. Dreaming of an owl may suggest that you need to trust your instincts when making decisions.

Rabbit: Rabbits usually represent fertility, abundance, and luck. They can also suggest that it is time for you to take a leap of faith to achieve success.

Rat: Rats can be seen as symbols of fear, disease, and danger. However, they can also represent adaptability and resourcefulness, allowing you to overcome obstacles.

Snake: Snakes are often seen as a symbol of transformation and spiritual growth. They can also warn you that danger or temptation is nearby, so be careful.

Tiger: Tigers represent boldness, courage, and determination. If a tiger appears in your dream, it may be time for you to draw upon these qualities within yourself to achieve success.

Wolf: Wolves are often seen as symbols of protection, guidance, and loyalty. If a wolf appears in your dream, it may mean that someone close to you will help lead you on the right path.

Numbers

One: Symbolizes unity, completion, and the beginning of something new. It can be seen as a milestone or the start of an adventure.

Two: Represents relationships, partnerships, balance, and duality. It can also refer to choices that must be made and being caught between two options.

Three: Refers to creative expression and growth. It symbolizes potential and is associated with self-expression and optimism.

Four: Associated with stability and security in life and feelings of being grounded and rooted in one's universe.

Five: Represents change and transformation, both internal (personal development) and external (environmental changes).

Six: Refers to harmony and balance. It often symbolizes the need to create a harmonious environment or situation to reach one's goals.

Seven: Associated with spiritual growth, inner wisdom, and intuition. It can also represent achievements and success.

Eight: Symbolizes abundance, prosperity, and self-confidence.

Nine: Represents life cycles, renewal, endings, beginnings, and closure of old chapters in life. It can also be a sign of new opportunities or new beginnings.

Ten: Represents completeness and wholeness that comes from achieving success after hard work and dedication. It is seen as a sign of destiny and the end of a cycle.

Eleven: Is associated with spiritual enlightenment, divine guidance, and higher awareness. It can also indicate one's spiritual path or journey.

Twelve: Symbolizes inner strength, faith in oneself and the universe, and personal power. It signifies greater insight and understanding of one's life purpose.

Thirteen: Represents intuition, prophetic dreams, visions, and the ability to see beyond the physical realm. It can also symbolize transformation and ascension.

Fourteen: Signifies good luck, success, and having everything one needs in life. It can also be seen as a reminder that help is on its way.

Fifteen: Refers to independence and freedom from past limitations or beliefs holding someone back. It signifies manifesting positive change in one's life.

Sixteen: Associated with personal growth and development, reaching new levels of understanding, wisdom, and enlightenment.

Seventeen: Represents inner strength, perseverance, and courage. It can also symbolize hope and self-empowerment.

Eighteen: Symbolizes the cycle of life and the completion of one's journey. It can signify spiritual fulfillment and enlightenment.

Nineteen: Refers to renewal, healing, and forgiveness, both on an individual level and in relationships with others. It symbolizes personal growth and transformation.

Twenty: Represents stability, balance, and security in life, along with feelings of being grounded and rooted in one's universe. It can also indicate that help is on its way.

Plants

Daffodil: The daffodil signifies new beginnings, hopes for the future, rebirth, and resurrection.

Dahlia: A dahlia represents elegance, grace, dignity, inner strength, resilience, and optimism.

Daisy: The daisy symbolizes innocence, purity, youthfulness, optimism, and joy.

Hibiscus: The hibiscus signifies beauty, femininity, love, loyalty, and peace.

Hydrangea: The hydrangea represents gratitude, appreciation, understanding, harmony, and grace.

Ivy: Ivy symbolizes loyalty, friendship, longevity, strength, resilience, and determination.

Lily: The lily signifies purity, innocence, rebirth, rejuvenation, and life after death or renewal.

Lotus: A lotus represents enlightenment, spiritual awakening, divine power, inner peace, and harmony to those who contemplate its beauty.

Marigold: A marigold symbolizes passion, courage, and strength. In many cultures, it is seen as a flower that brings good luck and joy.

Orchid: An orchid signifies love, beauty, luxury, and wealth. Its exotic beauty makes it an ideal gift to give someone you love.

Rose: A rose represents love, beauty, perfection, passion, romance, and deep emotions.

Sunflower: The sunflower symbolizes optimism, hope, and good fortune. It is a reminder that even in the darkest times, light is always at the end of the tunnel.

Tulip: The tulip signifies abundance, fertility, and prosperity. It's also believed to bring good luck in many cultures.

Body Parts

Arms: Arms signify strength, comfort, protection, and the ability to carry out tasks in your life.

Back: Backs often represent support, strength, resilience in difficult times, and a need to look back at past experiences or turn back from something to move forward with greater clarity.

Brain: The brain is associated with intellect, problem-solving, and wisdom. A dream about the brain may suggest that you need to use your analytical skills or intuition to make sense of something happening in your life.

Ears: Ears often symbolize listening and paying attention to what others say. They could also suggest that you must pay more attention to your surroundings to understand the situations around you.

Eyes: Eyes symbolize insight and seeing things clearly. Dreams about eyes may indicate a need for clarity or insight into a situation you are facing in your waking life.

Hair: Hair signifies a need for self-expression, creativity, and a desire or an urge to stand out from the crowd.

Hands: Hands represent creativity, healing, the ability to complete tasks, and the need for control or authority over something.

Head: The head symbolizes intellect, wisdom, and the need to use your mind to solve a problem or figure out a solution.

Heart: The heart is associated with emotional connections, compassion, love, understanding, and a need for emotional healing or connection in your life.

Legs/Feet: Legs and feet signify movement, progress, a journey, feeling stuck in some area of your life, and a need to move forward to achieve your goals.

Mouth: Mouths may represent expression, communication, voice, and things you need to say but cannot express due to fear or other obstacles.

Nose: The nose often symbolizes intuition, knowledge, insight, or a need for increased awareness of yourself or the world around you.

Shoulders: Shoulders are associated with support, strength, resilience when dealing with difficult situations, and a need to take responsibility and be accountable for your actions.

Skin: Skin can signify vulnerability, sensitivity, insight, and a need to protect yourself from the outside world or to be more open and accepting of others.

Stomach: The stomach can represent digestion (literally and metaphorically), security and stability, and nourishment on an emotional level.

Teeth: Teeth symbolize communication, the ability to express oneself in different situations, and a need to be more mindful of what you say or how you say it.

Conclusion

Dream deciphering is a powerful tool that can lead to deep personal insight, offering you the opportunity to explore your subconscious mind. Through dream interpretation, you can identify certain recurring patterns in your thoughts and behaviors, as well as get an understanding of your life experiences and relationships with others. Exploring the depths of your subconscious mind and understanding its hidden messages through dreams is an exciting process that can be a powerful tool for personal growth.

After reading this book on dream interpretation, you have the necessary skills to decipher different elements that may appear in your dreams and interpret their symbolism. You have a good idea of what it means to dream about places, animals, plants, colors, and body parts. Armed with a deeper level of self-awareness through dream interpreting techniques such as free association and dream journaling, you can discover more about yourself and how you experience the world around us.

In addition to uncovering vital details about one's self, it is critical to note that dreams are often an attempt by our brains to process difficult emotions or memories that have been repressed. By understanding these symbols in your dreams, you can begin to heal from past traumas or unresolved issues. It's also important to remember that dreams are not always literal interpretations of events or feelings; they may be more abstract or symbolic representations of experiences. Therefore, it's crucial for individuals seeking clarity surrounding a dream interpretation to approach them with open-mindedness and curiosity.

Finally, anyone attempting to decipher their dreams needs to treat their journey with care and respect. Although some interpretations may be uncomfortable or even painful at first, people on this spiritual journey should learn to trust their intuition and allow themselves time for reflection before making any drastic changes based on their newfound knowledge. Dream interpretation does not need to be an intimidating or overwhelming experience; rather, it should be viewed as an opportunity for growth and personal discovery through which you can reach greater levels of understanding both within yourself and concerning others around you.

Through this book, readers can finally make sense of those mysterious dreams that have been recurring in their lives. Your dreams are now accessible for further exploration, helping bring a greater understanding of yourself and where you want to go in the future. May this book help bring clarity and purpose to your life—so keep dreaming!

Here's another book by Mari Silva that you might like

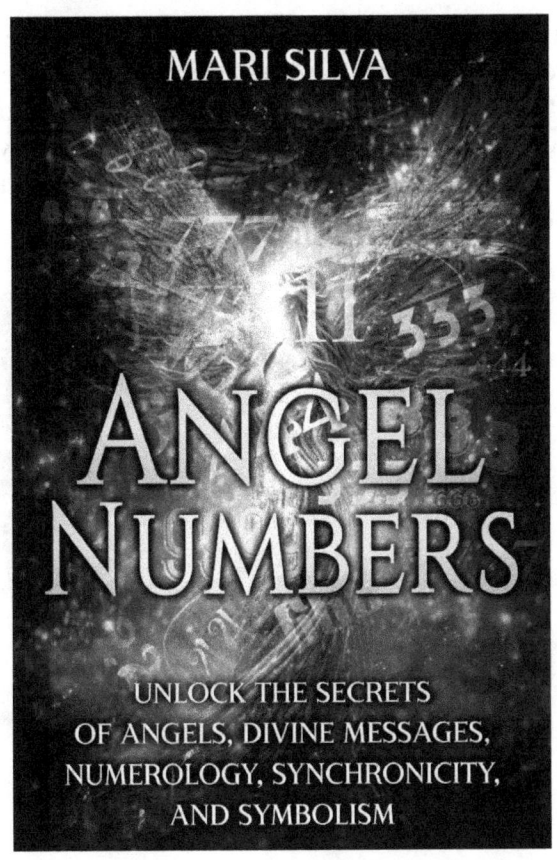

Your Free Gift
(only available for a limited time)

Thanks for getting this book! If you want to learn more about various spirituality topics, then join Mari Silva's community and get a free guided meditation MP3 for awakening your third eye. This guided meditation mp3 is designed to open and strengthen ones third eye so you can experience a higher state of consciousness. Simply visit the link below the image to get started.

https://spiritualityspot.com/meditation

Bibliography

AloDreams. "11 Dreams About Childhood Home – Meaning & Interpretation. Accessed April 1, 2023. https://alodreams.com/dreams-about-childhood-home.html

Alodreams.com. "#19 laughing – Dream Meaning & Interpretation." Accessed April 1, 2023. https://alodreams.com/laughing-dream-meaning.html

Alodreams.com. "#98 Dreams about Detached body parts – Meaning & Interpretation." Accessed April 1, 2023. https://alodreams.com/dreams-about-detached-body-parts.html

Angel Number. "Tunnel – Dream Meaning and Symbolism." Last modified March 17, 2021. https://angelnumber.org/tunnel-dream-meaning/

Apsara. "Falling in Your Dreams – Interpretation and Symbolism." Symbol Sage. Last modified September 28, 2022. https://symbolsage.com/falling-in-dreams-meaning/

Apsara. "What Does It Mean to Dream of Drowning?" Symbol Sage. Last modified September 26, 2022. https://symbolsage.com/dream-about-drowning/

Barber, N. "What Do Dreams of Numbers mean?" Dreams Limited. Last modified October 17, 2022. https://www.dreams.co.uk/sleep-matters-club/what-do-dreams-about-numbers-mean

Barber, N. "What Do Dreams of Water Mean?" Dreams Limited. Last modified June 17, 2022. https://www.dreams.co.uk/sleep-matters-club/what-do-dreams-of-water-mean-2

Barber, N. "What Do Ghost Dreams Mean?" Dreams Limited. Last modified December 13, 2021. https://www.dreams.co.uk/sleep-matters-club/what-do-ghost-dreams-mean

Basalt Spiritual. "12 Spiritual Meanings When You Dream About Drowning." Last modified December 8, 2022. https://www.basaltnapa.com/dream-about-drowning/

BetterSleep. "Dream Journals Explained." Last modified September 13, 2022. https://www.bettersleep.com/blog/dream-journal/

Björklund, Anna-Karin. "Do You Remember Numbers In Your Dreams? Here's What They Mean." Mindbodygreen. Last modified March 7, 2020. https://www.mindbodygreen.com/articles/what-does-dreaming-of-numbers-really-mean-heres-what-to-know

Brown, J. "What Does It Mean if You Dream About Flying?" ShutEye. Last modified July 16, 2021. https://www.shuteye.ai/dream-about-flying/

Brown, J. "What Does It Mean When You Dream About Falling." ShutEye. Last modified June 8, 2021. https://www.shuteye.ai/dream-about-falling/

Bulkeley, Kelly. "Jung's Theory of Dreams: A Reappraisal." Psychology Today. Last modified March 23, 2020. https://www.psychologytoday.com/us/blog/dreaming-in-the-digital-age/202003/jung-s-theory-dreams-reappraisal-0

Casale, Rebecca. "How To Remember Your Dreams." World of Lucid Dreaming. Accessed April 1, 2023. https://www.world-of-lucid-dreaming.com/how-to-remember-your-dreams.html

Chakraborty, S. "Dreaming of Laughing – Enjoy the Good Times of Your Life." ThePleasantDream. Last modified May 25, 2023. https://thepleasantdream.com/dreaming-of-laughing/

Cherry, Kendra. "How to Interpret Dreams." Verywell Mind. Last modified February 23, 2023. https://www.verywellmind.com/dream-interpretation-what-do-dreams-mean-2795930

Christian, A. "8 Stairs Dream Interpretation." DreamChrist. Last modified December 24, 2020. https://www.dreamchrist.com/stairs-dream-interpretation/

Christian, A. "9 Beach Dream Interpretation." DreamChrist. Last modified April 2, 2020.. https://www.dreamchrist.com/beach-dream-interpretation/

Christian, A. "10 Laughing Dream Interpretation." DreamChrist. Last modified September 19, 2020. https://www.dreamchrist.com/laughing-dream-interpretation/

Christian, A. "15 Church Dream Interpretation." DreamChrist. Last modified April 7, 2020.. https://www.dreamchrist.com/church-dream-interpretation/

Christian, A. "10 Amusement Park Dream Interpretation." DreamChrist. Last modified November 6, 2020. https://www.dreamchrist.com/amusement-park-dream-interpretation/

Christian, A. "Forest Dream Interpretation." DreamChrist. Last modified November 11, 2020.

https://www.dreamchrist.com/forest-dream-interpretation/

Cummins, Pamela. (2017, June 8). "12 Benefits of Dream Interpretation." Last modified June 8, 2017. https://pamelacummins.com/2017/06/08/12-benefits-of-dream-interpretation/

Daphne. "Dream Of The Amusement Park? 7 Fun Reasons." Daphne Den. Last modified October 19, 2021. https://daphneden.com/dream-amusement-park/

Derisz, Ricky. "How To Boost Your Dream Recall For Higher Creativity." Goalcast. Last modified June 4, 2022. https://www.goalcast.com/how-to-boost-your-dream-recall-for-higher-creativity/

Donovan, Melissa. "Journal Prompts for Dreamers." Writing Forward. Last modified June 16, 2020. https://www.writingforward.com/writing-prompts/journal-prompts/journal-prompts-for-dreamers

Dream Dictionary. "Church Dream Meaning." Last modified May 18, 2020. https://www.dreamdictionary.org/dream-dictionary/church-dream-meaning/

Dream Dictionary. "Dreaming Of Angels." Last modified November 4, 2021. https://www.dreamdictionary.org/dream-meaning/dreaming-of-angels/

Dream Dictionary. "Dreams About My Childhood Home." Last modified March 26, 2021. https://www.dreamdictionary.org/meaning/dreams-about-my-childhood-home/

Dreams, J. I. "12 Dream Interpretation Techniques to Understand Your Dreams." Journey Into Dreams. Last modified August 12, 2022. https://journeyintodreams.com/dream-interpretation-techniques/

Dreams, J. I. "City Dream Symbol Meaning." Journey Into Dreams. Last modified July 22, 2018. https://journeyintodreams.com/city-dream-symbol-meaning/

Dreams, J. I. "The Meaning of Colors: Color Symbolism in Our Dreams." Journey Into Dreams. Last modified July 16, 2020. https://journeyintodreams.com/colors/

Dream Meaning. "Fairy Dream Meaning Interpretation." Last modified July 13, 2019. https://www.dreammeaning.xyz/fairy-dream-meaning-interpretation/

Flo Saul. "Beach." Auntyflo. Last modified October 4, 2012. https://www.auntyflo.com/dream-dictionary/beach-0

Flo Saul. "Dream of Amusement Park." Auntyflo. Accessed April, 2023. https://www.auntyflo.com/dream-dictionary/amusement-park

Flo Saul. "Dream Of Childhood Home." Auntyflo. Accessed April 1, 2023. https://www.auntyflo.com/dream-dictionary/dream-of-childhood-home

Flo Saul. "Dreams About Animals." Auntyflo. Accessed April 1, 2023. https://www.auntyflo.com/dream-dictionary/dreams-about-animals

Flo Saul. "Dreams About Church." Auntyflo. Accessed April 1, 2023. https://www.auntyflo.com/dream-dictionary/dreams-about-church

Flo Saul. "Dreams About Drowning." Auntyflo. Accessed April 1, 2023. https://www.auntyflo.com/dream-dictionary/drowning

Flo Saul. "Dreams About Running." Auntyflo. Accessed April 1, 2023. https://www.auntyflo.com/dream-dictionary/dreams-about-running-meaning-interpretation

Flo Saul. "Dreams Of Earth." Auntyflo. Accessed April 1, 2023. https://www.auntyflo.com/dream-dictionary/earth-and-earthquake

Flo Saul. "Forest." Auntyflo. Accessed April 1, 2023. https://www.auntyflo.com/dream-dictionary/forest

Flo Saul. "Laughing." Auntyflo. Accessed April 1, 2023. https://www.auntyflo.com/dream-dictionary/laughing

Flo Saul. "Library." Auntyflo. Accessed April 1, 2023. https://www.auntyflo.com/dream-dictionary/library

Flo Saul. "Passages or Halls." Auntyflo. Accessed April 1, 2023. https://www.auntyflo.com/dream-dictionary/passages-or-halls

Flo Saul. "Uncover Hidden Dream Meanings." Auntyflo. Accessed April 1, 2023. https://www.auntyflo.com/dream-dictionary/countryside

Floyd, L. "4 Things That Our Dreams Tell Us about Ourselves." Landofsleep. Accessed April 1, 2023. https://www.landofsleep.com/blog/4-things-that-our-dreams-tell-us-about-ourselves

Forneret, Alica. "Dream of Running Meaning: 18 Scenarios." Last modified April 2, 2023. https://alicaforneret.com/dream-of-running/

Forneret, Alica. "Dreams About Ghosts Meaning: 13 Scenarios." Last modified January 17, 2023. https://alicaforneret.com/dream-about-ghosts/

Forneret, Alica. "Flying Dream Meaning: Spiritually, Psychologically & More." Last modified April 17, 2023. https://alicaforneret.com/flying-dream-meaning/

GoodTherapy. "Dream Analysis." Last modified February 2, 2016. https://www.goodtherapy.org/learn-about-therapy/types/dream-analysis

Home Science Tools. "Elements: Earth, Water, Air, and Fire." Last modified October 6, 2017. https://learning-center.homesciencetools.com/article/four-elements-science/amp/

Jiang, Fercility. "The 20 Most Common Animals in Dreams & Meanings." China Highlights. Last modified August 23, 2021. https://www.chinahighlights.com/travelguide/culture/dreaming-about-animals.htm

Jones, Walter. "Dream About Dragon: Meaning & Spiritual Messages Explained." Psychic Blaze. Last modified February 6, 2023. https://psychicblaze.com/dream-about-dragon-meaning/

Kari Hohne. "Anatomy and Body Parts." Accessed April 1, 2023. https://www.cafeausoul.com/oracles/dream-dictionary/anatomy-and-body-parts

Kari Hohne. "Animals." Accessed April 1, 2023. https://www.cafeausoul.com/oracles/dream-dictionary/animals

Kedia, S. "Dreaming about a library – Are You Actively Seeking Knowledge?" Last modified May 31, 2023. https://thepleasantdream.com/dreaming-about-a-library/

Kerkar, Pramrod. "Dream Therapy: Dream Interpretation, Why Do We Dream." Pain Assist. Last modified January 30, 2019. https://www.epainassist.com/alternative-therapy/dream-therapy-dream-interpretation-meaning-of-dreams-its-benefits

Kiran. "What Does it Mean to Dream About Running?" Dreams & Myths. Last modified August 24, 2022. https://dreamsandmythology.com/dream-about-running/

Kotiya, Madhu. "Dreams in colour." Deccan Chronicle. Last modified June 10, 2018. https://www.deccanchronicle.com/amp/lifestyle/health-and-wellbeing/100618/dreams-in-colour.html

Ladyfirst. "What does it mean to dream of 4 elements?" Last modified June 30, 2023. https://www.lady-first.me/article/what-does-it-mean-to-dream-of-4-elements,6343.html

Liquids & Solids Spirit. "Dream About Sinking Ship? (7 Spiritual Meanings)." Last modified August 24, 2022. https://www.liquidsandsolids.com/dream-about-a-sinking-ship/

Lou. "What Does It Mean When You're Dreaming of Falling?" A Little Spark of Joy. Last modified February 21, 2022. https://www.alittlesparkofjoy.com/dreaming-of-falling/

Malory, J. "Earth, Air, Fire and Water in Dreams." Dreaming.Life. Accessed April 1, 2023. https://www.dreaming.life/dream-themes/earth-air-fire-and-water-in-dreams.htm

Master. "Basic Body Parts Dream Meaning – Common 64 Dreams About Body Parts." Dream Meaning Net. Last modified April 23, 2015. https://dream-meaning.net/life/basic-body-parts-dream-interpretation/

The Messenger. "Dream about Running Down A Hallway." DreamsDirectory. Last modified January 24, 2019. https://www.dreamsdirectory.com/dream-about-running-down-a-hallway-meaning.html

Miller's Guild. "12 Meanings When You Dream of Running." Last modified December 13, 2021. https://www.millersguild.com/dream-of-running/

Miller's Guild. "17 Meanings When You Dream About Eating." Last modified January 6, 2022. https://www.millersguild.com/eating-in-dream/

Mitrovic, M. "Dreaming of a Dwarf – Meaning and Explanation." Dream Glossary. Last modified September 25, 2020. https://www.dreamglossary.com/d/dwarfs/

More, R. "What Does the Number 9 Mean in a dream?" LoveToKnow Media. Last modified September 14, 2022. https://www.lovetoknowhealth.com/well-being/what-does-number-9-dream-symbolize

Nikita. "City Dream Meaning And Symbolism." Luciding. Last modified December 12, 2021. https://luciding.com/city-dream-symbol-meaning/

Numberogy.Com. "#14 Supernatural Dream Meaning & Spirituality." Accessed April 1, 2023. https://numberogy.com/supernatural-dream-meaning.html/

Nunez, K. "5 Lucid Dreaming Techniques to Try." Healthline. Last modified March 22, 2023. https://www.healthline.com/health/healthy-sleep/how-to-lucid-dream

O'Driscoll, Dana. "Dreaming Primer: Lucid Dreaming, Dream Recall, and Exploring Dreamscapes for Creativity." The Druids Garden. Last modified February 4, 2023. https://thedruidsgarden.com/2023/02/05/dreaming-primer-lucid-dreaming-dream-recall-and-exploring-dreamscapes-for-creativity/

Olesen, Jacob. "Color Meanings in Dreams: What Does Dreaming in Color Mean?" Color Meanings. Last modified December 11, 2014. https://www.color-meanings.com/color-meanings-in-dreams-what-does-dreaming-in-color-mean/

Parvez, Hanan. "Dreams about running and hiding from someone." PsychMechanics. Last modified April 25, 2022. https://www.psychmechanics.com/dreams-about-running-and-hiding-from-someone/

Pentelow, Orla. "The Meaning Behind Drowning In A Dream Is Just As Scary As The Dream Itself." Bustle. Last modified August 18, 2021. https://www.bustle.com/life/what-does-it-mean-when-i-drown-in-a-dream-while-its-likely-youre-stressed-there-is-upside-12708547

Porter, Liam. "Dreaming of Falling And What It Means." Dreams Limited. Last modified May 18, 2022. https://www.dreams.co.uk/sleep-matters-club/falling-in-your-dream

PsycholoGenie. "What Do Dreams About Stairs Mean and How to Interpret Them?" Accessed April 1, 2023. https://psychologenie.com/what-do-dreams-about-stairs-mean

Regan, Sarah. "A Beginner's Guide to Dream Interpretation & 8 Common Dreams." Mindbodygreen. Last modified April 29, 2023. https://www.mindbodygreen.com/articles/beginners-guide-to-dream-interpretation

Simwa, Adrianna. "Eating in the dream - what does it mean? Dream interpretation." Legit. Last modified September 19, 2018. https://www.legit.ng/1191964-eating-dream.html

The Sleep Diary. "10 Common Dreams About Stairs and Their Meanings." Last modified June 3, 2022. https://thesleepdiary.com/dreams-about-stairs/

Steber, Caroline. "7 Dreams About Falling, Decoded." Bustle. Last modified June 8, 2021. https://www.bustle.com/wellness/dreams-about-falling-meaning-experts

Surolia, K. "Dreaming of Plants – Does It Mean Growth Like Plants in Life?" ThePleasantDream. Last modified June 8, 2023. https://thepleasantdream.com/dreaming-of-plants/

Tamara. "Laughter in a Dream – Meaning and Symbolism." Dream Glossary. Last modified December 8, 2021. https://www.dreamglossary.com/l/laughter/

Tommy, M. "What Do Tunnels Mean In Dreams? – Beginning of A New Chapter in Your Life." ThePleasantDream. Last modified June 21, 2023. https://thepleasantdream.com/what-do-tunnels-mean-in-dreams/

What Dream Means. "What Does it Mean to Dream About Childhood Home?" Last modified March 5, 2021. https://whatdreammeans.com/what-does-it-mean-to-dream-about-childhood-home/

Wille. "The Ultimate Guide to Dream Interpretation." A Little Spark of Joy. Last modified May 9, 2023. https://www.alittlesparkofjoy.com/dream-interpretation

www.ingramcontent.com/pod-product-compliance
Lightning Source LLC
Chambersburg PA
CBHW051848160426
43209CB00006B/1211